YOUR
MONEY
AND
YOUR LIFE

YOUR MONEY
AND
YOUR LIFE

The High Stakes for Women Voters in '08 and Beyond

◇ ◇ ◇

Martha Burk

A.U. PUBLISHING
AUSTIN, TEXAS

Your Money *and* Your Life:
The High Stakes for Women
Voters in '08 and Beyond

Published by A.U. Publishing
Austin, Texas 78726

Copyright © 2008 by Martha Burk
First printing March 2008

Ordering information:
Quantity sales.
Baker & Taylor, Inc
http://www.btol.com
2550 West Tyvola Road, Suite 300
Charlotte, NC 28217
Phone: 800.775.1800; 704.998.3100
Single copies and smaller quantities
Feminist Majority Online Store
http://store.feminist.org
FMF Support Center
1155 US Highway. 17 South
Elizabeth City, NC 27909
Phone: 1-866-462-6321; Fax: 1-252-331-1728

Library of Congress Control Number: 2008923918

ISBN 1-4196-9021-3
ISBN 13: 978-1-4196-9021-1

9 8 7 6 5 4 3 2 1

Cover design by Michel Cicero & Brandi Phipps
Printed in The United States of America
Distributed by Baker & Taylor and BookSurge Direct

TABLE OF CONTENTS

ONE

Your Money *and* Your Life: What's at Stake?

Too often an election will be dramatically characterized as the "election of the century," or "the most important election in our lifetime." But this time it may be true.

In the past eight years, the U.S. has gone from record surpluses to record deficits. We are at war in two countries with no end in sight. Gasoline prices have doubled since 2000. Our country has been flooded with contaminated consumer products, including the toys our children play with, and our food supply is becoming less safe. Climate change is threatening the planet, yet the government is unresponsive.

But most importantly, women's rights, for which we fought so hard in the 20th century, have been steadily eroded since 2001. The first federal abortion ban in history became law in 2007. Title IX, the law requiring equal educational opportunities for girls and women, has been weakened.

A woman-hostile Supreme Court has seriously curtailed our right to challenge employment discrimination. The pay gap remains, and we are the only industrialized country on earth without some form of pregnancy leave or paid family leave.

The child care system in the U.S. is a patchwork of "make-do" arrangements that leaves families struggling, and the few federal child care programs that exist have been cut to the bone. Social Security, women's main retirement program, remains under pressure, and long-term care is an increasing problem that families must solve on their own.

There are many other pressing national issues we don't normally think about as "women's issues" – but that is indeed what they are. The economy, the wars in Iraq and Afghanistan, the health care crisis, tax policies – all affect women in different ways than they affect men, and all are growing concerns.

If this sounds like a doomsday scenario, it's not, though it is a challenge. *Women have the opportunity in 2008 to take control and make the changes needed in the elections and beyond* – but having the opportunity is not enough. We must have the will – firmly grounded in essential knowledge. That's what this book is about.

This book is not about any candidate or party. It's about the challenges we face from the setbacks of the last eight years, and what we can do about them going forward in 2008. But please don't think of this as just another "good citizens vote" sermon. Voting doesn't help, and indeed can hurt, if you vote against your own interests because you don't know the facts.

It is still true that knowledge is power. By the time you close this book you will know what's at stake for women as we go through this most important election and the next four years. But knowing won't bring change without action – and that means holding candidates and elected officials accountable for long-term solutions.

The first action we must take is confronting candidates – incumbents and challengers of both parties – with questions about their voting records and intentions on our most vital issues. At the end of each chapter in this book, you will find just such questions. If they're not exactly right for your candidate or region, they will help you think of others.

> "We shall employ agents, circulate tracts, petition the State and national Legislatures, and endeavor to enlist the pulpit and the press in our behalf."

These words are contained in the final paragraph of the *Declaration of Sentiments* from the First Women's Rights Convention held in 1848. The ladies of 1848 were determined, and after 72 more years of struggle they got what they wanted most – the vote. If they were alive to exercise that right in 2008, they might put it this way:

> Read their records. Go to town hall meetings and confront them. Call in when you hear them on the radio. If they don't mention women, ask why not. Spread the word when they say something about our issues, good or bad. Email. Blog. Raise hell. Forget fancy speeches and red-hot rhetoric. Arm yourself with knowledge and *vote your own interests.*

Those who would roll back the progress we've made in reaching economic, social, legal, and political equality have vast financial resources, are very well organized, and are too often driven by a misogyny that borders on outright hatred of women. They are not prone to participate in rational and reasonable discourse. They will usurp control of social policy at every opportunity. It's up to women to block them, and we must start *this year* in the election campaigns and in the voting booth.

How to Read This Book

The essential background you need to make a difference is found in the first six chapters of this book, so we urge you to read them first. After that – well, women have differing concerns. So read the chapters about your priority issues first. We do think there are eye-opening facts in every section, but skipping around won't hurt. It is not necessary to go straight through to get the most out of *Your Money* and *Your Life*.

When you're finished, we urge you to pass this book along, or keep it for reference and urge your friends to get a copy and read it too. After all, one woman *can* change the world – but it's easier if you work in groups.

TWO

Women Can Control Any Election: The Gender Gap

When the Constitution was adopted in 1789, the ruling class was white, male, and land-owning, and rights of full citizenship were granted on that basis. It was never disputed that"persons" granted citizenship were understood to be white and male, but the framers could not agree on whether land ownership should also be a requirement for voting. Unable to resolve the issue, they left voting requirements to the states. None of the states allowed Indians, black men, or any women, to vote.

The Fourteenth Amendment, ratified three years after the abolition of slavery in 1868, granted citizenship to "persons born or naturalized in the United States," and the right to vote to non-white men, but to no women, white or non-white. It also guaranteed "equal protection under the law," to all "persons."

The breathtaking hypocrisy of the federal government proposing a constitutional amendment guaranteeing equal protection for all citizens, while denying the female half the vote, was not lost on the suffragists. In the years before adoption, controversy raged as to whether women should be included, with the formidable Susan B. Anthony on the side of women (black and white) and the equally formidable Frederick Douglass against. Douglass's arguments were summed up by the influential newspaper editor Horace Greeley when he told the women:

> ... hold your claims, though just and imperative .. . in abeyance until the negro is safe beyond perad-venture, and your turn will come next. I conjure you to remember that this is "the negro's hour," and your first duty now is to go through the State and plead his claims.[1]

It went without saying that he meant *male* Negroes. Ultimately the guys won (surprise!), introducing the word "male" into the Constitution for the first time, and enshrining in that document that race discrimination is more serious than sex discrimination – a strange and enormously harmful notion that continues to be upheld by the courts to this day.

Women would have to work another 52 years, until 1920, to pass a separate amendment to get equal voting rights. Carrie Chapman Catt, one of the movement leaders, told just how hard it was:

> To get the word "male" in effect out of the Constitution cost the women of the country fifty-two years of pauseless campaign ... During that time they were forced to conduct fifty-six campaigns of referenda to male voters; 480 campaigns to get Legislatures to submit suffrage amendments to voters; 47 campaigns to get State constitutional conventions to write woman suffrage into state constitutions; 277 campaigns to get state party conventions to include woman suffrage planks; 30 campaigns to get presidential party conventions to adopt woman suffrage planks in party platforms; and 19 campaigns with 19 successive Congresses.[2]

There were too many arguments against women's suffrage to count, but a frequent one was that women did not need the vote because they would just vote as their husbands did anyway. Anti-suffragists feared that women would take over the nation and its politics. As a matter of fact, neither has happened. For the next sixty years, women did not even register to vote in the same numbers as men.

But in the 1980 election, a funny thing happened. Women outnumbered men in the population in general, and that year they surpassed men in both voter registration and turnout. *And for the first time in U.S. history, women voted in a markedly different way than men.*

The Equal Rights Amendment (ERA) granting equal constitutional rights to women was pending before the states, and the right to abortion had been upheld by the Supreme Court only seven years before. Ronald Reagan, the Republican candidate, ran on a platform that included opposition to both abortion rights and the ERA. His opponent, Democratic incumbent Jimmy Carter, was pro-choice and a strong ERA advocate.

Reagan won the election, but his support split along gender lines, with 54% of men voting for him vs. 46% of women – a difference of eight percentage points. The gender gap was identified and named by feminist political analyst Eleanor Smeal, and it has never gone away. Neither has women's majority in voting – that's why change is possible.

Though it has never gone away, since 1980 the gender gap has been larger in some elections than others. It was smallest (with women favoring Bill Clinton by 3%) in 1992, when third party candidate Ross Perot siphoned votes from both major party candidates. The gap was largest in 2000 – women favored Al Gore over George W. Bush by 12 percentage points – in a contested election that was awarded to Bush by the Supreme Court with a 5-4 decision.[3]

Women's votes have made the deciding difference in a number of other close elections, most recently contests in 2006 that turned over control of the Senate and the House of Representatives from majority Republican to majority Democratic. Black women provided the winning margin (a gender gap of 10 points) for Jim Webb, the anti-war Democrat challenging incumbent Republican George Allen in Virginia. Webb's victory produced a Democratic majority in the Senate.

If men had been the only voters, the Senate would still have a Republican majority, and new Senators John Tester (D-MT) and Claire McCaskill (D-MO), would not have been elected.

Everyone also knew that if the Democrats took the majority in the House of Representatives, the first woman in history would be Speaker of the House, Nancy Pelosi of California. Women saw this as much more important than men (54% – 43%).[4]

Voting is not the only place where gender gaps have developed. There are also gender gaps on issues, with women having different priorities than men. According to a poll commissioned by *Ms.* magazine and the Women Donor's Network (WDN) two days before the 2006 elections, female voters differed from

Issue	Women	Men	Gender Gap
Iraq War	54%	43%	11%
Health Care	46	33	13
Economy/Jobs	41	30	11
Social Security/ Retirement	40	31	9
Women's Equality	34	26	8
Minimum Wage	31	22	9
Child Care	30	20	10
Abortion	19	28	9
Katrina Rebuilding	30	17	13
Stem Cell Research	25	16	9
Paid Sick Leave	16	10	6

Ratings of 'Very High' Priority

men in both party affiliation and on the issues. Women identified as Democrats more often (44% –39%); percentage ratings on issues, by women and men, are shown in the following table, "Ratings of 'Very High' Priority."

Clearly, if women did not vote at all or voted in lower numbers than men, different people would be elected and different priorities would be emphasized by lawmakers.

Female elected leaders have been responsible for making a difference in Congress on a variety of issues, from efforts to end the war to pushing for more money for breast cancer research and combating violence against women.

Women are often in solidarity across party lines, and differ with men in their own parties. In the House of Representatives, Democratic women are decidedly more liberal than Democratic men.[5]

In the House's vote in May of 2007 to approve a bill authorizing supplemental funding for continuing the war in Iraq without benchmarks for withdrawal, women accounted for about 26 percent of the "no" vote, even though they comprised only 16 percent of the members of the House. In all, 53 percent of the women members of the House voted against open-ended funding of the war, compared to only 29 percent of the male representatives.

Votes on social issues are even more telling. Sixty four percent of the women in the Senate voted against the passage of the first federal abortion ban in history that became law in 2007, while 64% of the men in the Senate voted for it.[6] The women's vote did *not* split along party lines – both Democratic and Republican women voted against the ban. It seems obvious that if there had been more than 14 women in the Senate, the measure could have been defeated.

These examples are just a small snapshot of why gender gaps do matter – whether in the voting booth or in the halls of Congress. If women want to make change, they must vote their priorities regardless of party, and they must vote for candidates who share those priorities – again regardless of party. The good news is that women are now a permanent majority – in the population, in voter registration, and it voter turnout. That means women can control any election.

Wouldn't it be great if the fears of the anti-suffragists weren't so far-fetched after all?

THREE

Who's in Charge? Why Does it Matter?

The Guy (or Gal) at the Top . . .

We learned in civics classes that we have three branches of the government – the Executive (the president and his staff, including the Cabinet, advisors, and other political appointees), the Judicial (courts and judges), and the Legislative (the House and Senate) – and that the three have equal power and serve as "checks and balances" on each other. That's all true – up to a point. A great deal depends who is in charge of each branch at any given time.

In 2006, when answering a question about conduct of the Iraq war, President George W. Bush declared "I am the Decider." While pundits have often made light of the remark, the fact is that it's true a lot of the time. And most of the time it matters a great deal.

Though the Constitution grants the power to declare war only to Congress, in reality it is presidents who decide. The president also gets to decide (with the Advice and Consent of the Senate, which too often is a rubber stamp) who will sit on the courts, and which individuals will head the Cabinet departments.

Through these appointments, the president sets an agenda for the country, because appointees usually carry out their duties in accordance with the "Decider's" wishes. (The Supreme Court is sometimes an exception. Presidents mostly get who they want – if not the first choice then the second – but justices sometimes change their outlook over time. Of course, they're appointed for life and can't lose their jobs.)

Some people think that the government pretty well rocks on regardless of who is in the White House. After all, it's a huge bureaucracy, each department has its mission, and it may seem like not much changes from administration to administration.

But that view is wrong. It matters enormously, although all of the effects may not be visible to the general public. Consider some of the consequences – good and bad – of presidential agenda-setting and appointments in recent administrations:

Ronald Reagan

Anne M. Gorsuch, Environmental Protection Agency Director	A firm believer that the federal government, and specifically the EPA, was too big, wasteful, and too restrictive of business. Gorsuch cut the EPA budget by 22 percent. She boasted that she reduced the thickness of the book of clean water regulations from six inches to a half-inch.[7]
Clarence Thomas, Equal Employment Opportunity Commission Director	Downsized the agency and all but eliminated class action suits for employment discrimination. Let 9,000 age discrimination complaints lapse. Declared that sexual harassment claims were not possible to support and not a priority for the agency.[8]

George H.W. Bush

Clarence Thomas, Supreme Court	Votes with the conservative majority to uphold a federal abortion ban, curb women's employment rights, and outlawed using race as a factor in school integration plans (these in a single year – 2007).
Antonia Novello, Surgeon General, first woman and first Hispanic to hold the position	Focused her attention on the health of women, children and minorities. She played an important role in launching the Healthy Children Ready to Learn Initiative. Worked with other organizations to promote childhood immunization.

William J. Clinton

Donna Shalala Secretary Health and Human Services	Raised child immunization rates to the highest levels in history; led the fight against young peoples' use of tobacco; created national initiatives to fight breast cancer, racial and ethnic health disparities and violence against women.[9]
Ruth Bader Ginsburg, Supreme Court	Consistent vote for the rights of women, strong believer in freedom of choice. Issued rare dissents from the bench in 2007 in the *Gonzales* federal abortion ban cases, and in the *Ledbetter* case which curbed women's employment rights.[10]

George W. Bush

Eric Keroack followed by Susan Orr, Health and Human Services Family Planning	Both opposed birth control, even though the office oversees $283 million in annual grants to provide low-income families and others with contraceptive services, counseling and preventive screenings.[11]
Wade Horn, Health and Human Services Assistant Secretary	Founded the National Fatherhood Initiative to promote marriage as the solution to poverty, then gave the group a $12.38 million contract. Openly stated his belief that 'the husband is the head of the wife just as Christ is the head of the church. Increased 'Abstinence Only' sex education funding in the schools to $176 million per year. Advocated that federal benefits, such as Head Start and subsidized housing, should only be available to children of married couples, not single parents.[12]
John Roberts, Chief Justice, Supreme Court, and Samuel Alito, Supreme Court	Both credited with sharply turning the Court to the right, joining in 5-4 majorities upholding a federal abortion ban without a health exception, curtailing women's employment rights, and turning back school desegregation.[13]

These high-level and highly visible examples are only a tiny fraction of the number of appointments each president makes. Presidents infuse all government departments with appointees that will carry out their philosophy. If that philosophy is fairness and good government, the public wins. If that philosophy is anti-government, punitive toward the poor, sympathetic to the religious right, the very wealthy, and corporations, women lose.

Majorities Matter – Congress and Its Committees

Most business in Congress is done through a committee system, meaning that a bill doesn't just magically appear on the floor of the House or Senate for a vote. Bills are introduced, then they go to a committee for consideration. This is far from an orderly process, and what happens next almost always depends on which party is in the majority. That's because seats on each committee are determined by which party is in control.

If the Republicans are in control, they will by definition have the majority of seats on *every committee*, and the chairperson of *every committee* will be a Republican. The opposite is of course true if the Democrats are in the majority. The chairperson and majority members have control, so they get to be the "Deciders" when it comes to which bills the committee will consider (and which bills it won't – those will "die in committee").

So back to that bill process. This is a shorthand explanation, but it will give you the basics. Suppose a bill is introduced that would overturn an existing law, such as Title IX, which guarantees equal educational opportunities for girls in any school receiving federal money. (Senator Jesse Helms introduced just such a bill to overturn Title IX three years after it was passed by Congress and signed by President Nixon in 1972.)

The bill is immediately sent to a committee that deals with education.

If the committee chair does not like the bill, it is never scheduled to come up for discussion – the fate of Helms' measure to abolish Title IX. If the chair of the committee likes the bill, and thinks it ought to go to the floor for a vote, he or she schedules *hearings*, where advocates and experts come and talk to the committee about the pros and cons. Then the committee takes a vote on whether to send the bill to the full body (House or Senate) for a vote.

But the struggle isn't over, because the next step is getting it on the voting calendar, which is essentially a priority list. And guess who decides where it goes on the calendar? *The leaders from the majority party*. If a bill is placed too far down on the calendar, the clock may run out on the legislative session before it ever comes up for a vote.

Committees have another very important function – oversight. That means if something is going on in the government that they believe bears investigation, they can call people before the committee to talk about it, and place them under oath if they want. Or not. And the "or not" is sometimes the more important part of the equation.

For example, when it became public in early 2006 that President Bush was conducting a program of wiretapping conversations of U.S. citizens without court warrants, the Chairman of the Senate Select Committee on Intelligence, Senator Pat Roberts (R-KS) refused to hold hearings to investigate the legality of the program. When the Democrats gained power in the mid-term elections, the Senate Judiciary Committee issued subpoenas to the White House, Vice President Dick Cheney's office, and the Justice Department after what the panel's chairman Patrick Leahy (D-VT) called "stonewalling of the worst kind" of efforts to investigate the wiretapping.[14]

Committees can also call people other than government employees before them to explain things that impact the public health, safety, or well-being.

Remember when the tobacco executives stood before a congressional committee in 1994 and swore under oath that they didn't believe tobacco was addictive? Congress was investigating whether tobacco should be regulated as a drug. And here's what happened to the investigation in 1996: "Since the 1994 tobacco hearings the Republicans have taken control of the government majority, and the committee that investigated the tobacco companies is now headed by Thomas Bliley, a Republican from Virginia and one of the industry's strongest supporters."[15]

Size (of the Majority) Matters – A Lot

The number one priority of women (and men) in the 2006 mid-term election was ending the war. According to all the polls, this was a the main factor in changing both the House and Senate from Republican to Democratic majorities. Several races, including the decisive Webb/Allen race in Virginia that gave control of the Senate to the Democrats, were clearly decided by the women's vote. But even though the Democrats now have control, they cannot end the war because they do not have enough votes. You might be wondering why not – they have majorities in both houses, don't they?

In the simplest case, for a bill to become law, it must pass each house of Congress by a simple majority, and be signed by the president. But if the president wants to veto a bill to prevent it from becoming law after the Congress passes it, the path to enactment is much harder – and this is indeed a situation where size matters.

Why? Two reasons: 1) not all members of a party can be counted on to vote together, so a few defections can make the difference between victory and defeat, and 2) a simple majority is not necessarily enough anyway, because if the president vetoes a bill (or is even planning to do so) a much larger majority than a simple 51% is required to override.

Overriding a veto takes a 2/3 vote in both houses. Most of the time, if party leaders know they can't override a threatened or promised veto, they won't even bring a bill up for a vote. (The exception is when they want to embarrass the other party or the president on a popular measure like the State Children's Health Insurance Program, which President Bush vetoed twice.)

The vote in November of 2007 on making continued funding of the war contingent on a timetable for troop withdrawal is instructive. Democrats had crafted such a bill, which passed the House by 218-203. But everyone knew the President was going to veto it, because he wanted the war money with no strings attached. So the real number of votes needed to pass a veto-proof measure was not a simple one-vote margin, but a super-majority (2/3 of those present), which is the number of votes needed to override. In this case that would have meant a 277 vote majority, *and* that majority would have had to hold up in the next round – a veto-override vote.

So while Democrats do have majorities in both houses of Congress, they are not strong enough to go against a determined President Bush and members of his own party that stick with him no matter what. (The 2008 Democratic majority in the Senate – counting two Independents that vote with them – is only 51-49).

Since presidents often personally lobby members of Congress on matters of importance to them, gaining enough new votes to override a veto is very hard. In October of 2007, the House passed the popular State Children's Health Insurance Program (SCHIP) by 265-159, with 45 Republicans joining the Democratic majority. President Bush vetoed the bill. When the House tried to override, the vote was 273 to 156 – 13 votes short of the two-thirds majority needed for an override.

In the Senate, the going can even rougher. While House rules determine the amount of time a bill can be debated before it must be brought to a vote, there is no limit to the time a bill can be debated in the Senate. That means a bill can be "filibustered," or debated so long that the other side gives up (the bill is literally "talked to death").

The only way to end a filibuster is through *cloture*, a motion to end a filibuster. Invoking cloture requires a vote by 3/5 of the full Senate. If cloture is invoked further debate is limited to 30 hours. (Cloture is not a vote on the passage of the piece of legislation, only on whether to end debate and bring the bill up for a vote.)

Obviously if one party has only a one-vote majority in the Senate, as the Democrats currently do, it is virtually impossible to get a winning cloture vote. In the unlikely event that this does happen, the bill still faces the veto-threat hurdle, and must pass by a 2/3 majority of those present in the Senate if the president plans (or has already carried out) a veto.

A prominent bill that ran into trouble in the Senate in late 2007 because of a failed cloture vote was the comprehensive energy bill that had already passed the House. Cloture failed in the Senate 53-42. The slim Democratic majority was not strong enough to overcome Republicans who objected to provisions of the bill that would not only strip big oil companies of tax breaks, but also require utilities to produce 15% of their energy from renewable resources.

Since the Democrats knew they couldn't get the bill to the floor for a vote without making changes, they gave in on both provisions, producing a weaker bill that environmentalists criticized as not going nearly far enough.[16]

All this means that "just a few seats" matter a great deal. If your incumbent "brings home the bacon" in road and bridge projects but votes against your basic rights on abortion, you can't look the other way. If a candidate promises to solve the mortgage crisis but stands against women's access to paid family leave or affirmative action in government contracts, don't ignore it.

Small majorities fail. Women must give pro-woman candidates a *mandate* – by electing them in great numbers, not by just one or two   .

The (Almost) Last Word – The Supreme Court

The job of the Supreme Court is to settle arguments about the law. They may be arguments about whether something like flag burning or the right to abortion is protected under the Constitution, arguments about whether laws passed by Congress are constitutional, or arguments between parties as to the interpretation of the laws.

Supreme Court appointments are extremely important, because they are for life. The decisions handed down are usually final, or at the very least can last for generations before new cases trigger a revisiting of a prior decision. Presidents appoint people to the Supreme Court that mirror the president's views about what the laws mean, or what they ought to mean.

Though everyone denies that "litmus tests" are used in appointments, this is simply not true. An anti-choice president is going to appoint anti-choice judges, and a pro-corporate president is going to appoint judges that he believes agree with him, whether or not the nominee is willing to say so publicly.

When it comes to women, Supreme Courts in the past have ruled that birth control is legal, that women have the right to abortion, that women have the right to equal educational opportunities, and that women have the right to be free from discrimination and sexual harassment at work, to cite just a few decisions.

But with new appointments of Justices Roberts and Alito to the Supreme Court under President Bush, the tide turned against women. The current Supreme Court has upheld a federal ban on one abortion proce-dure (with no exception for health of the woman), and severely curtailed the rights of women to take action when they learn they are being discriminated against in pay or promotion at work, overtuning over 40 years of precedent.

While the Supreme Court almost always has the last word, it can be overruled by Congress in some instances – such as those where the "intent" of a particular law is at issue. In reality, this happens very rarely, and it is no substitute for a court that upholds the rights of women in the first place.

Again, Title IX, the law prohibiting discrimination in education if an institution is receiving federal funds, is instructional. When the law was passed in 1972, Congress intended it to apply across the board to any program in an educational institution receiving federal money, regardless of where the money went. So women in a university couldn't be kept out of the law school, for example, even if all the federal money went to the medical school.

But in 1984, in a case called *Grove City v. Bell*, the Court issued a narrow interpretation of Title IX that opened a loophole. The justices ruled that colleges could discriminate against women in some programs (e.g. sports) if that particular program did not receive federal money, even if the school as a whole did.

Congress overturned the ruling four years later by passing a new law (the Civil Rights Restoration Act) explicitly stating that Title IX applies to all programs in any school receiving federal support, regardless of which department the money goes to.

But just because advocates succeeded after a four year fight in this case, don't believe congressional action is an easy or reliable safeguard against bad court opinions. As we saw above in the discussion of majorities and overrides, there is no guarantee that this process can succeed once the Supreme Court makes a ruling – most of the time Congress doesn't even try. That's why it is crucial that pro-woman judges be appointed to begin with.

The next president is likely to have more than one appointment to the Supreme Court, setting the course of law as it affects women for a generation or more. Justices Stevens and Ginsburg, reliable pro-woman votes, are age 87 and 74 respectively. Four others are in their late sixties to early seventies.

Over the next eight years, the president could appoint at least two and perhaps as many as six Supreme Court justices. If those justices do not believe in the basic rights of women, the right to abortion will be overturned, and the gains of the 20th century in protection against discrimination in employment, education, pregnancy, and credit could be rolled back or eliminated, one by one.

It goes without saying that women must be the "Deciders" as to who will be in the White House making these appointments, and who will be in the Senate confirming them.

FOUR

Where We Stand: We've Come a Long Way, But There's A Long Way to Go

There is no question that women in the United States, whether rich, poor, or in between, enjoy a relatively high standard of living compared to many women worldwide. But among developed nations, U.S. women are far from being "number one" politically and socially. If we are to change things at the ballot box, we first have to know where we really stand, both in our own country and in comparison to women in other parts of the world who live in industrialized countries with economies and governments similar to our own.

Below find a few quick facts. They may look like dry statistics, but they are eye-opening. You will see some of these again, and more, in this book under specific issues.

Constitutional Rights:

— Women do not have equal rights with men under the United States Constitution.

— Twenty-one U.S. states have equal rights guarantees in their constitutions.

— Most individual countries in Europe have formalized equal rights for women in their constitutions, and equal rights are included in the pending European constitution.

– Women have had equal constitutional rights in Japan since 1946, and the constitutions of many other countries worldwide declare women as legal equals to men.

– Since the 1990s, new constitutions in countries like Mozambique, Namibia, Ethiopia, Malawi, Uganda, South Africa, Rwanda, Burundi, and Swaziland have included non-discrimination or equality provisions, prohibiting customary practices if they undermine undermined the dignity, welfare or status of women.[17]

Political participation:

– In September 2006, the U.S. ranked 67th in the world in the number of women in Congress, with 15% of the House of Representatives and 14% of the Senate (increased to 17% and 16% in November 2006). By contrast, among developed countries, Sweden ranked the highest, with women making up 47% in Parliament.[18]

There are 74 countries where quotas for women have been implemented in the constitution, regulations and laws, or where political parties have implemented their own internal quotas.

– The United States has never had a female President, Vice President, Chief Justice of the

Supreme Court, or Senate Majority Leader. The first female Speaker of the House of Representatives was elected in 2006. In the 20th century, there were 46 female Prime Ministers or Presidents in other countries. At the end of 2007, there were 9 sitting female Presidents and 6 female Prime Ministers worldwide.[19]

– Women are the majority in the United States, and outnumber men in voter registration and voter turnout. In the 2004 presidential election, women voters made up 54% of the total.

Earnings, Pay Gap:

– Women working year-round and full time in the U.S. earn 77% of the wages men make overall. African-American women earn just 69 cents to every dollar earned by white men (the highest group), and for Hispanic women that figure drops to a mere 59 cents per dollar. Native American women get only 58 cents. Women in Australia, Belgium, Italy and Sweden earn 80%, and women in Austria, Canada and Japan earn about 60%.[20]

– Fifty-six percent of the nearly 37 million Americans living in poverty are female.[21]

– Adult women are nearly two-thirds of all U.S. minimum-wage workers. A woman with two children working full-time at the 2007 $5.85

federal minimum-wage lives nearly 30 percent below the poverty line.[22]

Workplace protection:

- Employers in the United States are prohibited by Title VII of the 1964 Civil Rights Act from discriminating on the basis of sex. The burden of proof that discrimination occurs falls on the worker. There is no protection against discrimination on the basis of sexual orientation.

- Women (and men) in the U.S. have no legal right to sick leave. This puts us in stark contrast to other countries – 145 provide paid sick days for short or long-term illness, and more than 79 give either 26 weeks or leave until recovery from illness.[23]

- There is no legal right in the U.S. for paid maternity or paternity leave. By way of comparison, out of 168 nations in a 2004 Harvard University study, 168 had some form of paid maternity leave, leaving the United States in the company of Lesotho, Papua New Guinea and Swaziland.[24]

- While U.S. law guarantees 12 weeks of *unpaid* family leave for birth, adoption, or family illness, we lag behind other countries in paid family benefits. Ninety eight of the 168 other countries that have guaranteed paid maternity leave offer 14 or more weeks off with pay, 66 provide paid paternal leave, and 37 ensure paid leave for illness of a child.[25]

Business:

– Though women make up almost half of the workforce, in 2007 there were 13 women heading Fortune 500 companies in the U.S. – 2.6%. Only one woman headed a Fortune 50 company. Women held less than 15% of the board seats overall, and more than 40% of the companies had two or fewer women on their boards. More than 10% had no women at all.[26]

– Even though the number of women business owners is growing at twice the rate of other businesses, a large gap still exists in the share of federal dollars going to contracts with women-owned businesses.

In 2007, only 3.3% of contracts were awarded to women-owned businesses. This represents a $5 billion shortfall in the share of dollars women owned business would have received if the government had reached its goal of 5%, set *more than twelve years ago.*[27]

In contrast, the top six recipients of federal contracts are Lockheed Martin, Boeing, Northrop Grumman, Raytheon, General Dynamics, and Halliburton. Collectively, they scooped up almost a quarter of all federal procurement spending, totaling $100 billion in 2006 alone.[28]

Higher Education/ Professions:

- Women now outnumber men in college enrollments, but they remain segregated by college
  major, with women making up 79 percent of
  education majors and men making up 82
  percent of engineering majors. This segregation
  is found in the workplace as well, where
  women make up 74 percent of the education
  field and the engineering and architecture
  fields are 84 percent male.

  And a pay gap exists despite the fact that
  women outperform men in school – earning
  slightly higher GPAs than men in every college
  major, including engineering, computer science, science and mathematics.[29]

- Women represented only a little over 16% of
  undergrads enrolled in science and engineering
  programs as of 2005, down from 17% ten years
  earlier.[30] The percentage of computer science
  degrees awarded to females is declining significantly – down from 38% in 1985 to only 28%
  in 2003. At universities that also offer graduate
  degrees in computer science, a mere 17 percent
  of the field's bachelor's degrees in the 2003-04
  academic year went to women.[31]

- Female enrollment in business programs is
  stuck at around 30%. According to the Graduate Management Admission Council, female
  students are more likely than men to carry
  educational debt prior to business school,

making business school a less affordable option for them than for men.

– Women are close to parity with men in law schools, but their numbers are dropping. Since 2002, the percentage of women in law schools has declined each year, according to the American Bar Association. Six years ago, women made up 49 percent of law school enrollment. In 2007, 46.9 percent of law school students were women. And while the number of applicants overall has dropped in the past two years, the percentage decline in the number of women has been greater.[32]

– Roughly 40% of medical school graduates are female. But many of the highest paid specialties, the ones in which salaries often exceed $400,000, remain dominated by men and based on the pipeline of residents, will remain so for decades to come.[33]

Child care:

– U.S. parents pay almost all of their child care costs without state or federal assistance, amounting to a large portion of household income (25% for families below poverty level).[34] This is the main reason why enrollment in child care and early childhood education is lower in the U.S. than in other industrialized countries.[35]

- Many countries in Europe have some form of national child care. For example, almost 100 percent of French three-, four-, and five-year-olds are enrolled in the full-day, free *écoles maternelles*; all are part of the same national system, with the same curriculum, staffed by teachers paid good wages by the same national ministry.[36]

- Most public child care funding in the U.S. goes to poor families – but only 14% of federally eligible children receive child care assistance. And we are going backward. Proposed cuts in federal child care spending would reduce the number of children *actually receiving* child care assistance from 2.5 million in 2003 to 2.3 million in 2009, out of over 15 million *eligible* children.[37]

Health:

- Eighteen percent of women in the U.S. lack health insurance. The numbers are miserable when broken down by race: 22% of African American women go without insurance, 35.9% of Native American women, and a whopping 37.8% of Hispanic women are not covered.[38] Virtually every country in Europe has universal health care, as do Australia, Canada, and Japan.

- Over 15% of U.S. women have no first trimester pre-natal care, and over one-third of U.S.

women live in a county without abortion services.[39]

– Women now account for more than one quarter of all new HIV/AIDS diagnoses. Women of color are especially affected by HIV infection and AIDS. In 2004 (the most recent year for which data are available), HIV infection was the leading cause of death for black women aged 25–34 years. In the same year, HIV infection the 4th leading cause of death for Hispanic women aged 35–44 years. The only diseases causing more deaths of women overall were cancer and heart disease.[40] The U.S. is only slightly better off than Ukraine, the country hardest hit by HIV/AIDS in Eastern Europe, where 30 percent of HIV infections are among women.[41]

Long-term Care:

– Women are the primary recipients of long-term care services. That's because older women tend to have chronic health problems and consequently require more long-term care services than men, whose illnesses tend to be acute and short-term.[42]

– The majority of *unpaid* family caregivers are women providing assistance to individuals, usually relatives, who need long-term care. Sixty percent are wives of disabled, often older, husbands. Most of these women are 65 and older, and many are facing their own aging, physical illnesses, or financial burdens.[43]

 — More than 90% of *paid* long-term care workers in the United States are female —about half are racial or ethnic minorities. Paid caregivers provide a remarkable array of services, while generally receiving low wages ($10 per hour or less) and few employee benefits.[44]

 — In the U.S., there are few government resources for long-term care of the elderly, except for some elderly poor. Long-term and elder care varies in other countries, but many, such as Japan and the Netherlands, provide for assistance regardless of income. In Canada, 8 of the 10 provinces now provide some form of long-term care coverage for all citizens.[45]

Social Security Benefits:

 — In the United States, both women and men are eligible for Social Security at age 62 (reduced lifetime benefit) or 65 (full lifetime benefit). Benefits are based on earnings of the worker (or if married earnings of the spouse if the spouse's income is higher). Wives or husbands who do not have an earnings record receive 50% of spouse's benefit. There is no credit for time out of the workforce for caregiving.[46]

 — In the United Kingdom, the number of work years needed for a full pension is reduced if the insured is caring for a child or an elderly or disabled relative.[47]

— In France, pensioners are granted a child-rearing supplement equal to 10% of the pension if the insured has reared at least three children.[48]

— In Japan, a survivor's benefit of 792,100 yen ($7,075) a year is paid for a widow. (No benefit is payable for a widower.)[49]

Violence:

— Fifty five percent of women in the U.S. will experience violence over their lifetime.[50]

— The U.S. ranks near the top in the world (9th) in the number of rapes per thousand population.[51] The vast majority of victims are female.

— According to the U.S. Department of Justice, on average in 2005 more than three women a day were murdered by their husbands or boyfriends in the U.S.

International Treaties Affecting Women:

— The United States is the only industrialized country that has not ratified the international bill of rights for women, called The Convention on the Elimination of All Forms of Discrimination against Women (CEDAW). By not ratifying, the U.S. is in the company of countries like Iran, Sudan, and Somalia.[52]

– The Convention on the Rights of the Child is the most widely accepted human rights treaty. Of all the United Nations member states, only the United States and the collapsed state of Somalia have not ratified it.[53]

– The Beijing Platform for Action for women adopted in 1995 by the U.N. Fourth World Conference on Women recognizes that women and children are particularly affected by the indiscriminate use of landmines. In December 1997, the treaty banning the use, production, trade and stockpiling of antipersonnel mines was signed by 122 countries.

Ten years later, 156 governments had ratified the treaty, including most members of NATO. Only 39 countries have not yet joined – including the United States, Russia, China, India and Pakistan.[54]

FIVE

What Do Women Want – Or At Least, What Are We Thinking?

Women and men often think alike, but when it comes to politics and priorities, the book title "Men are from Mars, Women are from Venus" is often true. That's because women's life experiences are different, and that causes them to see things in a different way than men. Gun control is a good example. When asked about how available guns should be, men might think of hunting, "cleaning up Dodge," or defending their households. Women think of getting raped at gunpoint or their children getting shot at school – a basic difference in point of view.

Even when women and men are on the same page, women may feel stronger about an issue (e.g. both rate the war in Iraq high on the list of priorities, but women are more passionate about it). And women and men often rank issues differently when it comes to what is most important.

We've already seen how gender differences play out at the polls. Looking at what women and men tell pollsters is one way to get behind the voting numbers, to see what drives the gender gap in the voting booth. It's also a way to get a good idea of the values and opinions that shape priorities – and how women and men might view the issues that should be addressed in 2008 and beyond by candidates and elected officials.

Are Women (and Men) Feminists?

The answer to this question seems to depend on whether women are asked about the *word* "feminist," or the *dictionary definition* of a feminist. When asked if they are feminists with no explanation – "Do you consider yourself a feminist? – only about a quarter of women say yes. But when asked the question this way – "A feminist is someone who believes in social, political, and economic equality of the sexes. Do you think of yourself as a feminist or not?" – 65% of women identify as feminists, and so do 58% of men.[55]

When asked to rate the importance of women's equality for Congress after the 2006 elections, over one third of women and twenty-six percent of men rated it a top priority.[56]

Women believe strongly that the women's movement has made their lives better, with 65% saying yes. Men are about evenly divided on the question – maybe because they now have to wash more dishes. When asked *how* the women's movement has made their lives better, women cite better jobs, more choices, better pay, and more legal equality.

Fifty-one percent of working women think there is still a need for a strong women's movement, compared to 39 percent of women who are currently not employed outside the home.[57]

Perhaps more women would think there is still a need for a strong women's movement if they realized that women do not have equal rights in the U.S. Constitution (see p. 227). In the most recent poll conducted on equal rights between women and men, 96% of Americans, regardless of their sex, age, race, geographic region, or other demographic category, said they believed that male and female citizens should have equal rights, and 88% stated that the U.S. Constitution should make it clear that they are so entitled. (There is a gender gap on this, with 85% of men and 91% of women saying the constitution should be clear on equal rights.) However, nearly three out of four Americans (69% of women and over 75% of men) assume that the Constitution *already* includes that guarantee – and they're all wrong.[58]

How Women Identify Politically

For a number of years, women have been voting in greater numbers than men, and choosing more Democratic than Republican party candidates, producing the now familiar gender gap at the polls. The numbers below (from exit polls of actual voters) show how people identify their political affiliation, with large numbers calling themselves independents.

Since 1972, both women and men have switched to the independent category from one or the other parties. Men have migrated away from calling themselves Democrats, with more moving to the independent category than to the Republican ranks. Females have been more stable, the majority identifying as Democrats since 1972, and fewer leaving either party to become independents.

As of 2006, there was an 11% gender gap in Democratic party identification between women and men (43%-32%). The gender gap between females and males identifying as Republicans was only 3%.

The table on the next page shows us how party identification has shifted over the years.

Party Identification
Year-by-Year Party Identification By Gender[59]

	Male			Female		
	Dem.	Ind.	Rep.	Dem.	Ind.	Rep.
1972	44%	22%	34%	47%	17%	36%
1976	39%	38%	23%	43%	30%	27%
1980	42%	27%	31%	48%	24%	28%
1984	35%	29%	36%	41%	23%	35%
1988	33%	28%	39%	42%	25%	33%
1992	34%	30%	36%	41%	26%	34%
1996	34%	29%	37%	44%	23%	33%
2000	33%	29%	38%	44%	25%	32%
2004	31%	29%	39%	41%	24%	35%
2006	32%	31%	37%	43%	23%	34%

National Priorities

In January, 2008 the Pew Research Center for People and the Press surveyed women and men on the nation's most important problems.[60] Respondents did not pick from a list, but could name anything they wanted to name, and they could provide multiple answers. There were significant gender gaps.

Just as they had before the 2006 elections, women still named the Iraq War as their highest concern, a 10 point gender gap over men, even though the economy had started to sour on the heels of the sub-prime mortgage crisis and dominated the news. Men did name the economy most often, a 6 point gender gap over women.

Both groups rated health care third, but women were far more concerned about it than men, with fewer than 10% of men saying it was the most important issue. Far down the list were terrorism, immigration, dissatisfaction with the government, unemployment, and education – 7% or fewer of respondents named any of them.

Nation's Most Important Problem

	Male	Female	Gender Gap	
Iraq War	22 %	32 %	+ 10	**
Economy	23 %	17 %	-6	**
Health care	8 %	13 %	+ 5	**
Immigration	7 %	6 %	-1	
Dissatisfaction with govt.	7 %	5 %	-2	
Unemployment	5 %	6 %	+ 1	
Education	3 %	4 %	+ 1	

** Statistically significant gender gaps

Women, consistent with their rating the Iraq war as their highest priority, are also backing away from global involvement. Only 37% completely agree that " it's best for the U.S. to be active globally," compared to 47% of men – a 10 point gender gap.[61]

In a separate part of the 2008 Pew survey, people were read a list of top priorities for President Bush and Congress, and respondents were asked whether they considered a given issue a "top priority." The results are found in the table that follows.

Top priorities for Bush and Congress

	Male	Female	Gender Gap	
Strengthening economy	76 %	75 %	-1	
Defend from terrorist attacks	73 %	75 %	+2	
Reducing health care costs	64 %	73 %	+9	**
Improving job situation	59 %	64 %	+5	
Dealing with energy problem	63 %	56 %	-7	
Reducing budget deficit	61 %	55 %	-6	
Protecting the environment	55 %	57 %	+2	
Reducing crime	49 %	60 %	+11	**
Health insurance for uninsured	48 %	60 %	+12	**
Deal with problems of poor	45 %	57 %	+12	**
Reducing middle class taxes	48 %	45 %	-3	
Make tax cuts permanent	36 %	35 %	-1	

**Statistically significant gender gaps

It is interesting to note that when respondents were read a list of potential priorities, "defending from terrorist attacks," came out second for both sexes, but it didn't make the list at all when people were asked to name their own top concerns without being prompted.

It is also remarkable that the pollsters did not include "Ending the Iraq War" in the list, given that it was the number one issue in the 2006 elections (75% of voters rated it high or very high in importance),[62] and also number one with the majority (women) when they were asked the open-ended question.

In terms of priorities for the president and Congress, there were significant gender gaps in the percentage of women (60%) vs. men (49%) rating "reducing health care costs" as a high priority. Similar gaps were found on reducing crime, getting health insurance for the uninsured, and dealing with problems of the poor, with significantly more women choosing these as a top priority. Both women and men rated "making the [Bush] tax cuts permanent" lower than all of the other concerns.

Economic Issues

A separate part of the Pew survey asked about national economic conditions and personal financial situations. Though not many people rated the economy "excellent" overall, twice as many men did so as women.

Less than a third rated the economy either "excellent" or "good," with women, who suffer more from a weak economy, producing a significant 6 point gender gap. Women also rated their personal financial situations worse than men.

National Economic Conditions	Male	Female	Gender Gap	
Excellent	4 %	2 %	-2	
Good	25 %	21 %	-4	
Excellent/Good combined	29 %	23 %	-6	**
Only fair	42 %	47 %	-5	
Poor	29 %	28 %	-1	

Personal Financial Situation	Male	Female	Gender Gap	
Excellent	12 %	8 %	-4	**
Good	40 %	39 %	-1	
Only fair	31 %	37 %	-6	
Poor	15 %	15 %	–	

**Statistically significant gender gaps

These results are consistent with other polls going back to the 2006 elections, when women rated a number of economic issues higher in importance than men did. An election-eve poll conducted by Lake Research Partners for *Ms.* magazine and the Women Donors Network asked people to assign a number of 0 (very low priority) to 10 (very high priority) to the several economic issues:[63]

Percent Rating "10" in importance

Issue	Men	Women	Gender Gap
Economy/Jobs	30	41	11
Social Security & Retirement	31	40	9
Raising Minimum Wage	22	31	9
Paid Sick Leave	10	16	6

It is not surprising that women put raising the minimum wage and Social Security higher than men did. The majority of minimum wage workers are adult women, and women depend on Social Security as their main retirement program in much higher numbers than men, who more often have private pensions.

Affirmative action is linked to whether or not women are given good educational and job opportunities, therefore it is related to economic issues. Given the fact that the gender pay gap is persistent and the ranks of women thin considerably as they go up the job ladder, it is not surprising that women strongly support affirmative action.

While support for affirmative action is strongest among blacks (93% – no gender breakdown available), support among white women and men is also quite solid. Even so, we see a gender gap: white men favor affirmative action programs by a large majority (65%) but white women are even more supportive (71%). Over all groups, support has grown by 12 points since 1995.[64]

Women (and Men) Are Pro-Choice

Public divisions over access to abortion are long-standing, and have changed only slightly over the past two decades. Both women and men in the U.S. are pro-choice, with only small gender differences.

In 2008, women say abortion should be legal in all or most cases by 58%, and men agree (54%). Extremely large majorities (80% or above) of both sexes say abortion should be legal to save a woman's life or health, and in cases of rape or incest.[65]

In a poll conducted by The Pew Research Center for People and the Press in April 2004, 58% said they opposed making it more difficult for a woman to get an abortion; just 36% were in favor of further restrictions.

The 2006 election results bore this out – all state referenda restricting abortion were defeated. Despite an intense effort by conservatives to sway public opinion, the 2004 polling results were virtually unchanged the early 1990s.[66]

There are gender gaps between women and men on abortion, and there are also divisions between women, depending on their point of view. Both pro-choice and anti-choice women expressed significantly stronger feelings about the issue, and much more often said it could be a factor in their vote.

An analysis of recent Pew surveys finds that 33% of women said they strongly opposed more restrictions on abortion, compared with 26% of men. On the other side of the issue, 19% of anti-choice women strongly favor greater restrictions, compared with 15% of men.

Taken together, the majority of women (52% overall) feel strongly about the issue one way or the other, while only 41% of men say the same – a gender gap of 11 points.

Women's greater concern about abortion is also seen in the extent to which they see it as a voting issue. On the anti-choice side, a plurality of women who favor more restrictions (45%) said they would not vote for a candidate who disagreed with them – a significant difference from anti-choice men (37%).

The gender gap is somewhat larger on the pro-choice side, where 40% of women and just 30% of men who opposed further limits on abortion said they would decide their vote largely on this issue. Overall, men who oppose more abortion restrictions are the least likely to view this as a voting issue.

Nearly six-in-ten men who oppose further abortion restrictions (59%) say they would vote for a candidate who disagrees with them on this matter, if they shared views on most other issues.

There also is a sizable gender gap in abortion attitudes among younger adults. Women age 18-24 oppose further limits on abortion access by a wide margin (63% oppose -34% favor). But young men are more closely divided – 50% of those polled opposed more abortion restrictions, while 45% were in favor.[67]

In terms of activism, women seeking more restrictions on abortion are somewhat more active. They stand out as one of the groups most engaged in the debate, with 21% reporting that they have actively expressed their views through donations, activities or letter writing in the previous year.

Only 13% of women who opposed abortion restrictions had taken similar steps. On both sides of the issue, men are less likely to have done anything to express their views.[68]

Women are More Supportive of Gay and Lesbian Rights

Public acceptance of same-sex relationships has increased in the past few years, and again we see gender divides on how people think about them. Though majorities of men and women now agree that "homosexuality is an acceptable lifestyle," women (61%) are more supportive than men (53%) – an 8 point gender gap.[69]

There are also gaps on specific issues. In January, 2007, women and men were polled on whether they favored or opposed allowing gay men and lesbians to marry legally. Women were more supportive overall (42% favored or strongly favored vs. 32% for men). Men were more against legalized gay marriage, with 60% opposing it vs. 49% of women.

Gender Views on Gay Marriage, January 2007[70]
Allowing gays and lesbians to marry legally

	Male	Female	Gender Gap	
Strongly favor	10%	16%	+6	**
Favor	22%	26%	+4	**
Oppose	24%	19%	-5	**
Strongly oppose	36%	30%	-6	**
Don't know/refused to answer	8%	9%	-1	

** Statistically significant gender gap

When women and men were asked about support for allowing gay and lesbian adoption, 50% of women favored, while only 41% of men agreed (both groups were more favorable than they were in 1999, when 43% of women and 33% of men were in support). Similarly, women are more supportive of allowing gays to serve openly in the military. Sixty-six of women are in favor, compared to 55% of men.[71]

Gender Gaps on Other Issues in the Public Debate

Political candidates and elected officials alike are prone to overstatement and red-hot rhetoric on certain social issues (see ch. 6 on false prophets) A few quick facts:

— Support for the death penalty for persons convicted of murder is somewhat lower now than it was in the late 1990s, but opinions have changed little since 2001. Currently, 64% favor the death penalty, while 29% oppose it. Support is higher among men (68%) than women (60%).[72]

— On gun control, there is a sizable gender gap (17-18 points) in opinions about whether incidents like mass school shootings are isolated acts of troubled individuals, or represent broader societal problems. By 55%-39%, men say that such shootings are just isolated acts. By a nearly identical margin (54%-37%), women believe these incidents reflect broader problems in American society. Mothers are significantly more likely than fathers to say they are trying to restrict how much television coverage their kids see on such incidents (46% vs. 32%).[73]

— Though neither women nor men rate expanding stem cell research as the highest priority for Congress, more women (25%) rate it that way than men (16%).[74]

— Sixty-two percent of Americans favor women serving in combat, and men and women are equally likely to support it. Politically, similar majorities of both Republicans and Democrats favor allowing women in the military to participate in combat.[75]

SIX

Politicians With Forked Tongues:
Beware the False Prophets

We know that women are the majority of voters, and can control any election. And we've seen what women care about. But do candidates and parties listen? Too often the answer is "no."

Candidates and parties, with a good deal of help from the media, are notorious for turning the debate in campaigns away from issues people are most concerned about in favor of topics that stir up emotional reactions, oftentimes while misrepresenting the facts.

A case in point was the CNN-YouTube Republican debate in December 2007, four weeks before the first caucus for the 2008 presidential nomination. Almost half of the two hour debate was devoted to immigration – though only 4% of the American people ranked immigration as the most important problem facing the country In the Democratic debate the next week, candidate Bill Richardson complained afterward that the war was barely mentioned – even though it was the number one issue with voters.

False prophet politicians concentrate on two categories: wedge issues and non-issues. Wedge issues are so-called "hot button" social issues, calculated to divide voters along false fault lines. They are almost always presented simplistically or outright dishonestly. Non-issues are those that actually affect only a small fraction of Americans, and either fall extremely low on the list of priorities for voters or do not register all.

Both categories could also be called "bait and switch" issues, because candidates talk a lot about them during the campaigns but do nothing once elected. (If they actually solved the "problem" they would not have the issue to run on again next time.)

I've listed some examples below. When you hear these come up, ask yourself, and the candidates, why they are talking about important issues in a misleading way, or why they seem obsessed with the non-issues while ignoring problems women really care about.

Wedge Issues

Banning Abortion: Conservative and religious right candidates often run with "ending abortion" as their number one priority, and say that's what the country wants. They present "abortion on demand" as a grave national problem, even though recent events indicate the opposite is true – access to abortion is more restricted now than it has been in the last 35 years, and the right to abortion is more threatened than at any time since it became legal in 1973 (see p. 97).

As for the voters, polls consistently show that both men and women are pro-choice, and do not want further restrictions on abortion (see p. 46). And while neither gender ranks abortion as one of their top five issues overall, there is a large gender gap in how important women see it as opposed to men. Forty-six percent of women rated abortion as a high priority for Congress after the 2006 election, as opposed to 38% of men.[76]

Constitutional ban on gay marriage: The rights of gay Americans to marry each other or form same-sex legal unions emerged in a big way in the 2002 elections, with conservative candidates stumping for a constitutional ban. President Bush took up the call in his State of the Union address of 2004. In 2006 conservatives placed bans on gay marriage and/or same sex unions on the ballots in eight states.

Seven passed, although by smaller majorities than in the past. The ban in Arizona was defeated by a 52% majority of voters, with senior citizens opposing the ban because it impacted shared living arrangements and property rights of cohabiting heterosexual couples.

While national polls indicate that a bare majority (51%) is still opposed to gay marriage, opposition has declined significantly from 63% in February 2004[77].

And no poll has shown that a federal anti-gay amendment has anywhere near the level of support needed to secure two-thirds approval in both houses of Congress and ratification by three-quarters of the states[78].

Women support gay marriage in greater numbers than men (41% – 31%)[79]. Fewer people oppose civil unions overall, and there is a larger gender gap; women are considerably more inclined to support civil unions than men (51%-39%).[80]

In any case, banning gay marriage through a constitutional amendment is extremely low on the priority list of most pressing issues facing the country — it doesn't make the list at all when pollsters ask the open-ended question "What do you think is the most important problem facing this country today?"[81]

When "Social issues such as abortion and gay marriage" is specifically included in a list of desirable top priorities for the federal government, only 3% choose that option.[82]

Deporting Immigrants/ Building a Fence: It is estimated that there are 12 million illegal immigrants in the U.S. today, and at least one million legal immigrants that are nevertheless not U.S. citizens (e.g. waiting for citizenship or with legal temporary work permits). Research has shown that politicians with the fewest immigrants in their states are the most prone to "grandstand" on the issue with punitive anti-immigration votes, since they don't actually have to deal with it[83].

Conservative candidates often hold that Americans want a "get-tough and get-tough-only" approach, but *public opinion research does not back them up*. The National Immigration Forum, after a compilation and analysis of polls from a number of sources such as *Time Magazine* and the Associated Press, concluded that the public wants a much less punitive solution, with "strong support for a more intelligent and realistic approach to controlling immigration, including enhanced border security, workplace and employer enforcement, earned legalization for undocumented immigrants with a path to citizenship, and expanded visas for future immigrant workers and families."

Majorities favoring citizenship for illegal immigrants if they learn English, have a job, and pay taxes reach as high as 78%.[84]

People on both sides of the aisle agree that our immigration policies are dysfunctional. However, debate continues over how to solve the illegal immigration problem, since the labor provided by these individuals is needed in many states.

Proposals range from creating programs whereby those in the country illegally can start on a path to citizenship (with variations on how to accomplish this), to extremely unrealistic plans for deporting them all wholesale and building a fence along the entire U.S. – Mexico border. (One wag asked how we can find 12 million people and deport them when we couldn't get one million out of New Orleans after Katrina, and we knew where *they* were.)

While most Americans have somewhat liberal opinions on how to solve our immigration problems, few rank it a priority for the country above other issues. When asked "What do you think is the most important problem facing this country today?" in December 2007, one month before the Iowa presidential caucuses and after hearing candidates and the press emphasize the issue for months, only 4% answered "immigration."[85] Even Republican pollsters admit that "[these same voters may be] just paying lip service to an issue they feel obligated to salute because of conservative media attention."[86]

Non-Issues

"Death tax": This is a term false prophet politicians use to describe the estate tax or inheritance tax. Candidates who grandstand on this issue would have us believe that we are all going to die paupers, and be unable to leave any of our hard-earned dollars to our children and grandchildren. In reality, the estate tax is relevant to less than one-third of one percent of all

U.S. estates[87]. That's .0033 of the population, 33 people out of every 10,000!

The term refers to the federal tax on estates over $4 million (for a married couple, or $2 million for an individual). But not the whole estate: a family's first four million is exempt. So repeal of the estate tax is of no benefit whatsoever to almost all Americans, because they are never going to reach the threshold for the tax in the first place.

While a few very wealthy families may indeed have some concern about the estate tax, it *never* gets mentioned by ordinary Americans when talking about their concerns and priorities – particularly not by women.

Gun Control: Gun control is another area where politicians like to posture. Many will falsely assert that the public wants *less* gun control, saying voters are fearful of losing their second amendment rights.

Though the numbers vary slightly from poll to poll, the majority of Americans in fact favor stricter gun control laws (though most don't want guns banned outright). Women want stronger gun control laws by a 70% majority, and 50% of men favor more controls.[88]

There is also a significant gender gap on whether the second amendment means that individuals have the right to own guns (men 72%, women 58%) as opposed to meaning that citizens have the right to form militias (men 26%, women 35%).[89]

But whether it is a top issue for voters and one they want to hear more about from candidates is another matter. When people are asked about their most important issues, gun control does not even make the list, even if respondents get to name more than one concern.[90] [91]

"Tort Reform": The term "tort reform" is used as shorthand for limiting the ability of individuals to bring lawsuits for medical malpractice, nursing home abuse, harm from tainted or unsafe products, personal injury at unsafe workplaces, insurance abuse, and other wrongs, and to limit awards when such suits are successful.

Conservative think tanks and politicians have relentlessly pushed the idea that the U.S. courts are hopelessly clogged because of "frivolous lawsuits," and that the awards are outrageously unfair to business.[92]

In fact, the majority of lawsuits are filed by businesses against one another and do not originate with individuals. And the public is far more concerned with corporate abuse of workers and the public, than with abuse of the courts by individuals.

An extensive poll of likely 2008 voters conducted by Peter D. Hart Associates in July of 2007 found that "Americans are deeply worried about their nation's future, and corporate misconduct is a major source of their anxiety."

Voters also considered corporate misconduct much more important than "lawsuit abuse." Trial lawyers making too much money and victims getting too much award money ranked at the bottom of a list of concerns, behind 11 examples of corporate misconduct.[93] Neither "tort reform" or "lawsuit abuse" is mentioned at all when people are asked to name their top concerns with open-ended questions about their own priorities, or priorities the government ought to address.[94]

The bottom line? Candidates should not be allowed to get away with grandstanding on wedge issues, or constantly harping on non-issues, to the exclusion of pressing national problems.

We've all heard the expression "buyer beware." You are the political buyer. Beware of false prophets.

SEVEN

Your Life, and Many Others: Ending the Wars

As we all know, the United States is currently engaged in two wars – one in Afghanistan and a much larger one in Iraq. The war in Afghanistan began in 2001, in retaliation for the attacks on New York and Washington September 11, 2001 by Al Qaeda terrorists. Afghanistan is known to shelter the group and its leader, Osama bin Laden.

Effect of the Wars on Women

At the time, women and girls in Afghanistan were being persecuted by the Taliban, the militia in charge of the country. They were denied basic human rights: not allowed to work or go to school, forced to wear head-to-toe burquas with even the eyes covered by mesh, and confined to their houses unless accompanied by a male relative. Women were stoned to death in stadiums filled to capacity, for infractions such as sex outside marriage.

President Bush promised to liberate the women, and some progress was made in the initial stages of the war. But women and girls are once more being persecuted as the Taliban have gained back much of the strength they lost immediately after the start of the war.

By 2006, girls' schools were routinely burned to the ground (by one estimate, one per day), and female teachers killed for "going against Islam."[95] The chief of women's affairs in Kandahar province was also assassinated in 2006, and female election workers, as well as those holding voter cards, have also been killed.[96] And women were back in the burqua in fear of their lives.

In a move that has shocked journalists and human rights activists around the world, in January 2008, an Afghan religious court sentenced a 23-year-old reporter and journalism student to death. His crime? Downloading information on women's role in Islam from the Internet and distributing it.

Iraq and Terrorists: What Connection?

Through the end of 2007, 475 American lives had been lost in Afghanistan, with 2007 being the deadliest year[97]. Bin Laden, the architect of the 9/11 attacks, has never been caught, and there is no end in sight for this war.

The invasion of Iraq by the United States began on March 19, 2003, after months of hype by the Bush administration claiming that Iraq had weapons of mass destruction and was an imminent threat to the U.S. These claims have been throughly discredited by both the United Nations and the U.S. government itself.[98] The Administration also repeatedly linked the attacks of 9/11 to Iraq, though there was no evidence that it was true.

Since the war began, however, Iraq has become a haven for terrorists from other countries. As husbands have disappeared or been killed in the fighting, women have lost much of their freedom to move about and hold jobs. Many have turned to prostitution to support themselves and their children.[99]

Public Attitudes

Initially support for the Iraq war was high, with 73% of the American people believing going to war was the right thing to do;[100] 70% believed that Iraq was complicit in the attacks of 9/11, though evidence was nonexistent.[101]

As the Iraq war wore on and the justifications for invading were discredited, the American public, led by women, turned against it. A large gender gap emerged, with 62% of men in 2004 wanting the U.S. to remain in Iraq, compared to only 45% of women.[102]

By the mid-term elections of 2006, 75% of voters overall cited ending the war as a top priority. It was once again more important to women, with 80% rating it very high as opposed to 71% of men.[103]

Since the Republicans in Congress continued to support the war, this was the biggest factor behind the voters (led by women, see p. 8) changing majority control in both the House and the Senate from Republican to Democratic.

The new majorities are not large enough to accomplish the goal, however. Democrats have not been able to institute a timetable for bringing the troops home, or to even tie continued funding for the war to such a timetable (see p.18). As of early February, 2008, 5,266 American lives had been lost in Iraq.[104]

The war in Iraq is still a very high priority for most voters of both parties; 68% of adults oppose it, and more people favor "withdraw all troops now," than any other option for ending the war.[105] Despite this, Republican candidate John McCain told ABC news during the 2008 primary season that the U.S. could be in Iraq for 100 more years.[106]

The Dollar and Social Cost

Besides the loss of life, the wars have been a major factor in the national budget deficit. President Bush took office with a surplus of over $171 billion.[107] The budget deficit in 2007 was $163 billion.[108] The war costs over $200 billion per year. That's half a million dollars *per minute* – and the impact of that cost on other spending has a great effect on what women and children can and cannot have.

The National Women's Law Center termed the 2008 budget "Millionaires First, Women and Children Last," citing cuts to programs that have been vital to human needs.

Starting in 2007, a wide range of domestic programs were scheduled to be cut or eliminated over the next four years under President Bush's budget. These included not only programs disproportionately affecting women such as education, child care, health research, and job training, but also such niceties as environmental protection.

Medicaid, primarily serving women and children, would be slashed by $26 billion, and recipients will have to meet higher premiums and co-payments to hang on to these meager health benefits-of-last-resort.

The president has proposed freezes on child care funding for the past six years, cutting almost half a million kids out of the program by 2010, according to his own proud estimates. And then there's food. Half of all food stamp participants are kids, and almost 70% of adults in the program are female, including 2/3 of the elderly who receive aid. Thanks to W, 231,000 recipients will lose this lifeline in a single year.

Last October, after he had requested $158 billion in spending for the wars in Iraq and Afghanistan for the year, the Senate was debating an appropriations bill for domestic education, labor and human services programs. President Bush a vetoed the bill – over a comparatively minor $11 billion[109].

At the same time, he was fighting Congress over reauthorizing the SCHIP bill, which provides health insurance for the children of working families. He vetoed it twice, calling it too expensive – even though it was to be 100% paid for, mostly by an increase in tobacco taxes.

With an annual tab of over $200 billion and counting, the money spent on *one day* of the war could buy health care for 423,529 kids, or buy homes for 6,500 families.

Looking at programs the president proposed zeroing out (though Congress saved some of them) in war dollars comes out this way: Commodity Supplemental Food Program providing food for expectant mothers, babies, and the elderly poor (the majority of whom are female), 3 ½ hours of the war; Maternal Child Health Grants, 1 hour, 18 minutes; Job Opportunities for Low Income Individuals, mostly women, 12 minutes.

When it comes to girls and women, no program is too small to escape the Bush meat axe. The tiny Women's Educational Equity Act – a program that helps get more girls into science, math, and technology – was also on the chopping block, though put back in the budget at the last minute by Congress. The tab in war dollars? *Six minutes.*[110]

Democrats vs. Republicans

Though there some are pro-war Democrats and a few anti-war Republicans, it's fair to say that the parties have opposite views on the need for continuing the war. Democrats in Congress want to end it, though they don't yet have strong enough majorities to make that happen over a presidential veto. Republicans have stuck with President Bush in voting to continue the war with no timetable for withdrawal.

There is serious disagreement between candidates and parties about the need to continue the wars indefinitely, though the public is solidly in favor of getting out. The impact of continued war spending, to the detriment of domestic programs that benefit women and children for years to come, puts much at stake in the outcome of the 2008 elections.

Questions for candidates:

Do you support the war in Iraq? How would you define "winning" the war in Iraq?

When would you begin bringing our troops home, and when would you have all of our troops out?

What do you think is being accomplished by the continuing war in Afghanistan?

Would you end the war in Afghanistan?

Women are being persecuted in both Iraq and Afghanistan, and not allowed basic human rights by the religious police. What would you recommend the U.S. do now to help women in those countries?

What would you do to ensure the rights of women in Afghanistan and Iraq after the U.S. involvement has ended?

EIGHT

Your Money: The Economy

Just what the heck *is* the economy?

For most people, economics is a word that scares them or causes their eyes to glaze over.

Economists throw around such terms as "demand curves," "elasticity," and "marginal utility" that most people have no clue about. Because ordinary citizens seldom understand these terms and the "economic theory" they come from, we are left to sort out the rhetoric of experts (many self-appointed), candidates, and elected officials about what is "best for the economy."

The discussion here won't make it into any economics textbook, and economists would undoubtedly judge it too simplistic, but it will give you an idea of what the arguments are about when various proposals are put forward about how to produce a sound economy. And when you finish this chapter, you will have the background and details necessary to understand what's at stake for women economy-wise in the the '08 elections and beyond.

The Personal (Economy) is Political

A simple dictionary definition of the economy is this: *the structure of economic life of a country.*

That's the dictionary definition. But for most people, the definition of the "economy" is very personal. If you and your family are doing well – you have a job at a living wage that allows you to buy the things you need, save for retirement and educate your kids without being terrified of the future – the economy is pretty good.

On the other hand, if you are unemployed or have a job that does not pay enough, you lack health insurance, can't pay for gasoline and the basics, much less save any money – then the economy for you is pretty bad, regardless of what is happening on Wall Street.

How're We Doing?

Your personal "economy" depends on how the overall economy in the country is doing. If the country is in an *expanding* economy, it means there are enough jobs and more are being created, more goods and services are being produced, and people have the money to pay for them.

Home ownership will be stable or on the upswing, and consumers will cannot only afford the basics, they will be able to buy extras such as a new television or a weekend vacation. This creates more jobs to produce these goods and services, resulting in more money circulating and continued economic growth.

Conversely, in a *shrinking* economy, job growth slows or employment actually declines, and layoffs will be on the rise. This results in less consumer spending as people tighten their belts in fear of or in reaction to job losses. As people buy less, demand goes down, so fewer goods and services are produced, which means lower profits leading to more layoffs and less personal and business investment.

The gross domestic product (GDP), a statistic issued by the Commerce Department, is the official measure of how well the economy is doing. The GDP totals up everything the economy has produced in the quarter, and tells how that figure has changed, on a percentage basis, from the previous quarter. A positive percentage change means the economy is growing; a negative one means it's shrinking. A GDP growth rate of 3% or more is considered robust.

A *recession* is when there has been a decline in the GDP for two consecutive quarters. When there is a recession (or even talk of one), consumers may become more wary and stop spending, even if nothing has changed much in their personal situations. That in turn can contribute to decline.

The Difference Interest Makes

Conservative rhetoric about "intrusive government intervention" notwithstanding, actions taken or not taken by the government have a great deal of influence over the economy.

One of the ways is in controlling interest rates, or how much it costs to borrow money. This is done through the Federal Reserve Bank (generally called The Fed), which can be thought of as a "bank for bankers." To keep the money supply flowing smoothly, the Fed loans money to other banks at a certain interest rate for short-term loans, called the "discount rate."

The discount rate that banks pay to the Fed influences the interest rate they charge their own customers. The discount rate is lowered from time-to-time to stimulate borrowing, or raised to dampen inflation.

As the discount rate goes up, banks have to pay more for money they borrow from the Fed, and in turn they have to charge more to businesses and consumers who borrow from them. That means interest rates on business debt, mortgages, car loans, and credit cards will go up.

When borrowers have to spend more on interest, they have less to spend on goods and services. Conversely, if the cost of borrowing is cheap, purchases that are financed effectively cost less, so businesses and consumers are inclined to spend more.

Lower rates and a healthy economy can also increase banks' willingness to lend to businesses and households. This may increase spending, especially by smaller borrowers who have few sources of credit other than banks. In a shrinking economy, the idea behind lowering interest rates is to get both businesses and individuals to be more willing to borrow and spend, thus stimulating economic growth.

For businesses, the reasoning behind lowering rates is pretty much the same as the argument for lowering taxes: make interest rates low, and businesses will borrow more to buy new equipment, open a new location, or upgrade their facilities.

This creates new jobs, and if more people are working they have more money to spend. They in turn pay more taxes, so the government can function without incurring more debt. Lowering interest rates is also thought to instill confidence that "things are going to be all right," arresting downward slides that are triggered by fear or talk of recession.

On the consumer end, low interest rates may induce buyers to buy more goods or buy more expensive things, since the interest rate is a big determinant of the monthly payments on credit cards, mortgages, and car loans.

A quick example: suppose you can afford a $500 per month payment for a new car. With a 10% annual interest rate and a three year loan, you can buy a car costing $18,000. But if interest is only 8%, you can go up to $18,500 and add some accessories for the same payment.

This is not necessarily bad, so long as interest rates remain stable. If you buy your car this year at the lower rate and the terms of your loan do not allow the rate to go up, then your rate is "locked in." If interest rates on new car loans go up next year, you won't be affected unless you want to buy another car.

But if interest rates go up on a loan you've already made so that the payments exceed the amount you budgeted, you may be in trouble. That is exactly what happened in the case of the sub-prime mortgage crisis that is widely blamed for triggering the 2008 recession.

The Mortgage/Housing Crisis

Subprime mortgages are high interest rate loans made to borrowers with low incomes or low credit scores – predominately women ("subprime" refers to the credit status of the borrower, not to the interest rate – which is very high). The loans make up 13% of existing home loans, but account for 55% of foreclosures.

Though women and men have roughly the same credit scores, women are 32% more likely to be sold subprime loans than men. Though this gender gap exists in every income and ethnic group, African-American women have been hit especially hard. Women do have less wealth than men, and that probably increases the likelihood they will be channeled into these loans.[111]

But plain old sex discrimination plays a role too. Institutions that buy loans from mortgage companies estimate that up to 50% of the subprime loans went to borrowers whose credit was good enough for standard rate loans.[112]

In the years leading up to the crisis, some lenders marketed subprime loans very aggressively with initial "teaser" interest rates that were low enough for borrowers to afford, but structured to increase greatly after the first few months or first year. In many cases house payments doubled.

Borrowers could not make the payments, so they defaulted on the loans and lost their homes. The number of mortgage defaults through fall 2007 were up 94% over the previous year, with entire neighborhoods virtually abandoned.[113] This in turn affected local and state tax revenues, forcing cuts in public services.

The crisis triggered increased scrutiny by bank regulators, who are supposed to protect consumers from dishonest or predatory lending practices (like Rip Van Winkle, they had been asleep from 2001 to 2006). As scrutiny was stepped up, banks tightened their lending practices, not only to consumers but also to businesses, making it harder for business to obtain loans for expansion and consumers to qualify for credit.[114]

As news coverage of the crisis exploded, people became more pessimistic and curbed spending, and "recession talk" in the media increased greatly. This prompted the Federal Reserve to lower interest rates drastically in January, 2008 to restore confidence and put the stop the slide.

But it was not enough to convince people – one month later 61% of the public said the economy was suffering through its first recession since 2001.[115] Congress, and belatedly the president, knew they had to act.

What Can Government Do?

When the economy slips into a recession or near-recession as it did in early 2008, both political parties get nervous, and propose various "fixes" to "get more money into circulation and stop the downward spiral. (It's unclear whether they're feeling the people's pain, or feeling the pain of trying to get elected in a downturn).

As unemployment goes up and production goes down, there is usually not much disagreement that a stimulus is needed to spur more buying and restore confidence – but there are serious and fundamental disagreements about what kind of fix it should be.

Debate over how to produce a healthy economy goes to the very heart of liberal/conservative philosophical divides. Conservatives put their faith in the business sector and the wealthy, while liberals and progressives believe government has a more direct role.

Since he took office in 2001, President Bush has had one solution to virtually every economic problem

– tax cuts primarily benefitting the wealthy. His philosophy is a simple-minded version of conservative arguments in general: if corporations and the wealthy individuals who fund them through investments pay lower taxes, they will invest those tax savings in ways that will create jobs, such as building new plants, acquiring new subsidiaries, or expanding product lines. Businesses will direct money to suppliers, contractors, and employees to accomplish these goals.

Trickle Down, or Trickle Up?

This theory has been generally referred to as "trickle-down," or "supply side economics," meaning change made at the top of the wealth pile eventually makes its way to workers at the bottom.[*] Corollaries are that private enterprise is always better than government spending, and the less government interferes in the "free market" through regulation, the better.

This theory sounds pretty good – if you believe the tax savings really will be spent on creating jobs instead of multimillion dollar bonuses for CEOs, fines and legal judgments for various abuses, or fatter dividends for stockholders. As for the expanding facilities and building new plants, that might indeed work as advertised – unless the facilities are already in China and the new plants will be in Mexico.

---

[*]The economist John Kenneth Galbraith noted that "trickle-down economics" had been tried before in the U.S. in the 1890s under the name "horse and sparrow theory": "if you feed enough oats to the horse, some will pass through to feed the sparrows."

Liberals and progressives believe that putting money in the hands of those that actually need it to live on is a better plan to keep the economy going – because they spend more of what they have instead of just adding it to stock and bond accounts. Very low income people have to spend it all – every month – just to buy the basics.

This school of thought would not replace the private sector, and in fact would agree that stimulating business in ways that actually creates jobs is good (e.g. removing tax incentives for moving jobs overseas).

Progressives also believe that the government can have a positive influence on economic growth through spending tax dollars. They would create some jobs by repairing infrastructure such as roads and bridges, funding green energy research and development, and restoring government services that have been cut.

They hold the principle that in a recession, money should be injected into the economy as fast as possible – even if the trickle down fantasy actually worked, the "tax breaks for business and the wealthy" scenario takes too long to do any good.

We saw the contrast in the these approaches in the debate over the stimulus package that President Bush signed in February, 2008. Democrats wanted to implement one-time tax rebates to working families, expanded unemployment benefits to those out of work, money to prevent home foreclosures, and assistance to state and local governments to stop public service cuts. Republicans at first insisted that making the Bush tax cuts slated to expire in 2010 permanent was the only fix needed.[116]

But as public pressure for a solution mounted, they agreed that a short term stimulus was warranted and the House passed a relief package (the entire House and 1/3 of the Senate was facing re-election – Bush wasn't).

Do You Feel Stimulated?

The House approved a $600 tax rebate check from the government ($1,200 for couples, plus $300 per child) for most workers, and for Social Security recipients who had income from a job or investments. in adjusted gross income for individuals and $150,000 for couples.

Workers making at least $3,000 who earn too little to pay personal income taxes would receive $300, plus $300 per child. Businesses got $45 billion in tax incentives, supposedly to invest in new plants and equipment.

The House bill included priorities of the Democrats (money directly to people who would spend it) and priorities of the Republicans (tax incentives for business). But the fundamental philosophical differences were more clearly evident in what the bill left out.

Democrats wanted payments for poor seniors whose only income was Social Security (more likely to spend it than rich seniors living on investments), extension of unemployment benefits (again more likely be spent immediately), and disabled veterans. Republicans wanted to remove the eligibility cap – meaning write checks to the wealthy – and make the 2003 tax cuts permanent. Neither side got these additional provisions.

Democrats in the Senate put up a fight to include the elderly poor and disabled veterans, an increase in monthly food stamp benefits, and an extension of unemployment benefits for those already out of work. They also wanted billions of dollars in energy tax credits and federally backed bonds for home construction.

Only the elderly poor and veteran provisions were added to the final House/Senate compromise. In exchange for those concessions, Republicans were allowed to insert language prohibiting illegal aliens from receiving any benefits.[117]

Women Win, Women Lose

Women were both winners and losers in the stimulus package. The provision adding benefits for the elderly who live solely on Social Security benefitted more women than men, because women are the majority of the elderly poor. Including low income workers with children who earn too little to pay taxes was also good for women, as this group is predominately single mothers.

Where did women lose? While there was much talk about the sub-prime mortgage crisis and indeed it was the initial impetus for the stimulus package, nothing was done to help, and in fact, the "fix" will probably hurt those that need it.

The stimulus package includes a provision to temporarily permit federally chartered mortgage companies (known as Fannie Mae and Freddie Mac) to buy or guarantee mortgages 75% higher than the current limit of $417,000. That puts them in the market for so-called "jumbo mortgages" held by the wealthy. Not only does it contradict their mission to "expand affordable housing," it could actually divert money away from less expensive housing which is caught in the mortgage crunch.

After the measure passed, the head of the Office of Federal Housing Enterprise Oversight pointed out to the Senate Banking Committee that funding one $600,000 mortgage takes as much capital as three $200,000 mortgages.[118] This means women will continue to lose their homes in disproportionate numbers as the mortgage interest rates reset to levels they can't afford.

The failure to include an increase in food stamp benefits was also a loss for women. Nearly 70 percent of adult food stamp beneficiaries are female. According to the National Women's Law Center in Washington, D.C., more money for food stamps would have been a particularly effective way to target the poor and boost the economy.[119] Benefits could be quickly deposited on debit cards and used almost immediately at grocery stores, providing an economic jolt and aiding women in particular.

Women further lost out in Congress' failure to include an extension of unemployment benefits, but they didn't lose as much as men – because women already get less out of unemployment insurance. Thirty-seven percent of jobless men draw benefits, as compared to 33 percent of unemployed women, according to the U.S. Department of Labor.

That's because the system was designed during the Great Depression, when men dominated the labor market. Unemployment benefits were crafted as a safety net for those who worked full time, met a certain income threshold, and lost their jobs solely because of an employer's decision.

Though women are now a permanent part of the labor force, fewer women than men meet these out-dated criteria because they are more likely to work part time or hold lower-wage jobs, making them less likely to meet the system's earnings thresholds. And women are more likely to leave their jobs because of domestic violence, harassment or stalking, to follow a spouse, or to take care of their families. None of these reasons for job loss are covered by unemployment insurance.[120]

All this says that whether or not extension of unemployment made it into the stimulus package, the system needs to be overhauled to reflect the economic reality of women's lives.

Women-Friendly Fixes

The Institute for Women's Policy Research in Washington, D.C. recommends several fixes.

> States can lower required earnings thresholds that currently exclude too many workers. Workers who lost a job and are looking for a part-time position can be granted benefits if they have sufficient earnings. And those who must leave work because of a caregiving crisis at home, such as a spouse becoming disabled or domestic or sexual violence, can also be deemed eligible if they meet earnings tests. All these workers have earned benefits, because unemployment taxes were contributed on their behalf while they were employed. In an

equitable, modern system, they would not be excluded by outdated rules and biases.[121]

Though economic slowdowns and recessions can be short-lived, they can also go on for many months and years. Long-term economic fixes are at stake in '08 and beyond. Whether the economy improves in the short run or not, women must hold candidates and elected officials accountable for long-term solutions.

Here are a few questions to help do that.

More and more women are losing their homes in the mortgage crisis, and the stimulus package did almost nothing to help. How would you stop foreclosures and keep women in their homes?

Do you think making the Bush tax cuts for the wealthy permanent will help the economy?

If you would vote to make the tax cuts permanent, what programs, specifically, would you cut to pay for it?

If the economy stays in a downturn, how would you help women who lose their jobs?

Would you expand eligibility for unemployment benefits to include more women, such as those who worked part time or had to leave their jobs to care of a disabled spouse or child?

If the economy stays in a downturn, would you increase food stamps?

NINE

Your Life: Reproductive Rights

Abstinence-Only Sex Education

Abstinence-only-until-marriage sex education is a term we've all heard, but many of us don't know much about it. It refers to a government-mandated method of teaching sex education to kids in schools accepting federal money from certain government programs (virtually all public schools and some private ones).

The mandate comes down to this: kids (and more recently adults up to age 29) can be taught *only* about abstinence until marriage as the way to avoid pregnancy, disease, and psychological and social consequences of having sex. In addition, they *must* be taught that marriage is the only appropriate context for sexual activity.

That's it – no birth control or protection against sexually transmitted disease, no medically accurate information about reproduction and child-bearing, and no acknowledgment that not everyone will marry and have children.

Most people think that abstinence-only-until-marriage sex education began under the second Bush administration, but the program actually dates back to 1981, when Ronald Reagan was in the White House. The Adolescent Family Life Act was crafted by conservatives to prevent teen pregnancy – by promoting *only chastity and self discipline.*

In those days, the programs also had a strong dose of religion. Specific religious references and providing classes in church sanctuaries were outlawed in 1993, after years of litigation. But federal money for abstinence-only continued to flow, and was increased dramatically in 1996, when $50 million per year was added by conservatives to President Clinton's high-priority welfare reform bill.

The new law, a provision of the Maternal and Child Health Block Grant (under Title V of Social Security), was groundbreaking, both for its funding level and also for its unprecedented, eight-point definition of abstinence education.

As you read the 8-point definition below, it might look pretty reasonable – some of it even good. But remember, the program is not *in addition to* any other sex education in public schools receiving funding under the program, it is *to the exclusion of* other programs, such as information about birth control methods. So schools taking the money (and few have refused) are forced to comply with this narrow definition of sex education under the law.

The Federal Definition of Abstinence-only Education[122]

An eligible abstinence education program is one that:

A. Has as its exclusive purpose, teaching the social, psychological, and health gains to be realized by abstaining from sexual activity

B. Teaches abstinence from sexual activity outside marriage as the expected standard for all school-age children

C. Teaches that abstinence from sexual activity is the only certain way to avoid out-of-wedlock pregnancy, sexually transmitted diseases, and other associated health problems

D. Teaches that a mutually faithful monogamous relationship in the context of marriage is the expected standard of human sexual activity

E. Teaches that sexual activity outside the context of marriage is likely to have harmful psychological and physical effects

F. Teaches that bearing children out-of-wedlock is likely to have harmful consequences for the child, the child's parents, and society

G. Teaches young people how to reject sexual advances and how alcohol and drug use increase vulnerability to sexual advances

H. Teaches the importance of attaining self-sufficiency before engaging in sexual activity.

At first, program guidance allowed grant recipients some flexibility in how they spent the money, and did not require that all eight elements of the definition be emphasized equally, though grantees could not provide information that contradicted any of the eight points. But by 2007, grant announcements stated that "each element of A through H should be meaningfully represented in all grantees' federally funded abstinence education curricula."

The latest grant announcement also required states to provide assurance that funded programs and curricula *do not promote contraception and/or condom use*.

In addition, the targeted population was redefined as "adolescents and/or adults within the 12 through 29-year-old age range." But the Bush administration was not content with this broad range. The newest age definition also included "other adults such as parents or professionals that desire training in how to support decisions to delay sexual activity until marriage."

Targeted groups (called "focal populations" in bureaucratese)also named were students at local universities, colleges, or technical schools, and single adults involved in a local community or community-based organizations.

To top it off, in a breathtaking demonstration of the disconnect between cause and effect, the new definition targeted
for abstinence- only- without- contraception- information "single parents in their 20s."

This tightening of program requirements, including the new directive to indoctrinate adults, has contributed to a small revolt against abstinence-only sex education. A few states have now turned down millions of dollars in federal grants.

The number of states that refused Title V abstinence-only funding grew from one (California) in the first year to nine in FY2008 (California, Connecticut, Maine, New Jersey, New Mexico, Montana, Ohio, Rhode Island, and Wisconsin).

Despite the mini-revolt, the vast majority of states are still accepting the money, and by definition complying with the restrictive requirements for teaching sex education in public schools.

Funding for abstinence-only has burgeoned under the Bush administration, going from $60 million a year to $176 million, and the 2006 budget noted that the request for abstinence-only programs will increase to a total of $270 million by 2008.[123]

To date, Congress has lavished over $1.5 billion in state and federal dollars on this ideologically driven and unscientific "sex education." Now, after almost a decade of extravagant and ever- increasing money injections, the government's own long-term research by the Department of Health and Human Services has clearly shown that abstinence-only programs do not delay sexual initiation, nor do they reduce rates of either teen pregnancy or sexually transmitted diseases.[124]

Not coincidentally, the teenage pregnancy rate rose in 2006 (the latest figures available) for the first time since 1991. Government officials were "surprised" but had "no immediate explanation." At the same time, sexually transmitted disease rates, including syphilis, gonorrhea, and chlamydia, have been rising.[125]

In sum, abstinence only programs began under a Reagan Republican administration, were increased somewhat under the Clinton Democratic administration (with Republican majorities in the House and Senate), and skyrocketed under George W. Bush.

Several attempts to end or cut back funding for abstinence only education by the Democrats in Congress failed in 2007, because they did not have veto-proof majorities in the House and Senate. Most notably was the Labor, Health and Human Services reauthorization in late 2007. Democrats had attempted to end Title V funding of the programs, but the entire bill was vetoed by President Bush. A vote to override in the House failed by 2 votes, demonstrating once again that size of the majority matters.

Questions for candidates:

Do you support comprehensive, age appropriate sex education in the public schools?

Do you think the federal government should mandate how sex education is taught in the public schools?

How have you voted, or how would you vote, on providing public school money for abstinence- only sex education?

Do you think our (state, school district) should take federal money for sex education if it restricts that education to abstinence only and nothing else?

Birth Control and Family Planning

Though some forms of birth control have been around for centuries, the legal history of birth control in the U.S. began in the 19th century. After Charles Good-year invented the vulcanization of rubber in 1839, rubber manufacturers began supplying not just condoms but douching syringes and "womb veils" (or diaphragms and cervical caps), and what amounted to intrauterine devices (IUDs).

By the 1870's, pharmacies were selling chemical suppositories, vaginal sponges and medicated tampons. All of these contraceptives were widely promoted in advertisements that were often detailed and graphic, giving us a disconcerting idea of some of the objects that women were encouraged to insert into their bodies.

Anthony Comstock, a onetime salesman in New York City and the philosophical father of anti-choice zealots today, believed birth control encouraged prostitution and fed the vice trade by separating sex from marriage and childbearing. He recruited others to his cause, and in 1873 they convinced Congress to pass a bill branding contraception obscene, and prohibiting its distribution across state lines or through the mails. Similar laws were passed in 24 states; they came to be known collectively as "Comstock Laws."

The Comstock laws did not do away with birth control – they merely led to it being marketed with the use of creative euphemisms describing " health devices" such as "married women's friends."

Though courts and juries often looked the other way, the Comstock laws remained in effect until 1918, when the spread of venereal disease in the armed forces of World War I became a concern. A New York appeals court ruled that contraceptive devices were legal as instruments for the maintenance of health.[126]

After the decision, states repealed their Comstock laws, except for Connecticut. The staunchly Catholic Connecticut legislature repeatedly refused to roll back its statute. By the 1960s, it was the only state with such a law, although other states regulated the distribution of birth control devices or banned birth control advertising.

The Planned Parenthood League of Connecticut had fought against Connecticut's prohibition for decades, and in 1965 they prevailed in the Supreme Court of the United States. The Court ruled in *Gris-*

wold v. Connecticut that the right of married couples to use birth control is protected as part of a right to privacy under the Constitution.

The federal government began to take an active part in providing birth control in 1967, when 6% of the funds allotted to the Maternal and Child Health Act were set aside for family planning. In 1970, President Nixon signed the Family Planning Services and Population Act (known as Title X), which established separate funds for birth control. Title X clinics offer low income women voluntary contraceptive services, prenatal care, treatment for sexually transmitted diseases (STDs), and other services.

Medicaid, the nation's joint federal/state health insurance program for the poor, has specified family planning services as a mandatory benefit since the Nixon administration in 1972. It also was one of the very few services for which patient cost sharing was prohibited– until the Deficit Reduction Act of 2006.

According to the most recent data available, nearly 12% of all women of reproductive age rely on Medicaid for their health care, and the program provides just over six in ten public dollars spent on family planning across the country.

But with the 2006 Deficit Reduction Act, states were allowed for the first time in more than 30 years to exclude family planning from the benefits offered to some groups of enrollees. In addition, they now may charge fees for at least some contraceptives or drugs used to treat sexually transmitted infections that are prescribed as part of a family planning visit.

The Guttmacher Institute, an organization re-searching reproductive health, says their data show that charging fees to poor women is a classic example of "penny wise and pound foolish." Many women cannot afford the co-pays, so will go without family planning services. To reduce both unintended pregnancies and abortions, programs should be expanded, not curtailed or eliminated.

California's experience is exemplary. The state's 2002 Medicaid family planning expansion prevented 213,000 unintended pregnancies, 45,000 of which would have been to teenagers. By preventing these pregnancies, the program helped women in California avoid a total of 82,000 abortions, 16,000 of which would have been to teenagers. And that's for just one year.[127]

International Family Planning

The influence of the U.S. on birth control and family planning policies and practices reaches far beyond our own shores. We are a major influence in what happens worldwide, including funding for birth control, accessibility of reproductive health services, and control of information about family planning.

International family planning has in fact become a "political football" in the U.S., with conservative Republican administrations cutting or eliminating programs altogether, and Democratic ones lending some support (see full discussion in chapter 22, Global Women's Issues).

President Bush's Fiscal Year 2008 budget request to Congress proposed cuts of 25%, not only to the United Nations Population Fund (UNFPA), but also to all U.S. programs promoting family planning and reproductive health overseas. This is in spite of the fact that maternal mortality remains high in many countries and more than 200 million women want, but cannot get access to, modern methods of family planning.

Other Family Planning Cuts

Cutting Medicaid and the UNFPA are not the only setbacks that have been delivered to family planning. Since 2000:

- On his first business day in office, President George W. Bush reinstated the Reagan-era "global gag rule," which prohibits the granting of U.S. funds to any overseas health clinic unless it agrees not to use its own, private, non-U.S. funds for any abortion related services. Since the main work of many of these clinics is birth control information, thereby reducing the need for abortion, women in poor countries have suffered. Lack of funds has caused many clinics to close altogether.[128]

- Though Title X has continued as a family planning program in the U.S., it has been funded far below the inflation rate. Conservatives in Congress have repeatedly tried to deny any of the funds to Planned Parenthood, one of the main family planning providers in the United States, because some clinics also provide abortion services.

– Information about condom use and efficacy was removed from the Center for Disease Control website.

– Approval of over-the-counter emergency contraception (commonly referred to as Plan B) was delayed until 2006, though the drug was approved by the FDA in 1998. Even then, it was approved without a prescription (but *behind* the counter) only for women over 18, who must show a photo ID to the pharmacist. Seventeen-year-olds and under need a prescription.

This effectively prevents access, since getting a prescription usually takes longer than the 72- hour window where the drug is effective, even if teens have insurance to pay for seeing a doctor and the wherewithal to do it. The rule also limits availability to immigrant women who may not have a government photo ID.

– Brand name prescription prices for birth control pills dispensed by campus clinics rose from about the $3 – $10 range per month to the $30 – $50 range as a byproduct of the Deficit Reduction Act of 2005. The law made it much more expensive for companies to offer schools the deep discounts on birth control that had kept pills affordable for college aged women.

– Eric Keroack, a doctor who believes the distribution of contraceptives is "demeaning to women," and who had a history of making outrageous statements, including that condoms "offer virtually no protection" against herpes or HPV, was appointed by President Bush to head U.S. contraception programs at the Department of Health and Human Services. The post has extensive power to shape the kinds of information disseminated to millions of women, develops guidelines for clinics, set priorities, and determine how scarce dollars get spent.

Family Planning, Insurance, and Pharmacies

One issue in the family planning debate is whether insurance plans that cover other drugs should also cover birth control pills. Women between the ages of 15 and 44 spend 68 percent more on out-of-pocket health costs than do men, much of it on contraception. Among that age group of women, birth-control pills are the most commonly prescribed drug.[129]

After Viagra came on the market, insurance companies (and Medicaid, which even supplied the drug to sex offenders)[130] quickly added Viagra to the list of covered drugs. There was an outcry from women, because most insurance does not cover birth control prescriptions. As a result, twenty-four of our fifty states now require insurers to cover prescription birth control if they cover other prescription drugs.

But once again, it's a piecemeal result. Coverage depends on what state a woman lives in, women are forced to fight for fairness one state at a time. Despite bipartisan sponsorship, the Equity in Prescription Insurance and Contraceptive Coverage Act (EPICC) that would mandate coverage in all the states, has languished in Congress since 1997.

Another birth control issue that has surfaced in the last few years is pharmacists refusing to fill birth control prescriptions if they are opposed to contraception. This so-called "conscience movement" is supported by such organizations as the U.S. Conference of Catholic Bishops and Pharmacists for Life International.

Pharmacists who refuse say they have a "moral right" to refuse the prescriptions, and some go so far as to refuse to refer women to other pharmacies.[131] This obviously jeopardizes or eliminates the right of women to obtain drugs that are legally prescribed, not to mention allowing pharmacists to veto women's private choices. There is no question that refusal to fill emergency contraception pills leads to delays that can result in unwanted pregnancy.

The battle is being played out at the state level so far, with a few states having laws on the books that require the prescriptions to be filled, and another handful having laws that say pharmacists don't have to do so. No federal action has been taken yet. "Access to Birth Control" bills have been introduced in both the House and Senate, but have not gotten hearings.

Since most of the activity on this issue is at the state level, it is particularly important that women ask any candidates running for state legislature where they stand. And ask yourself: how much sense does it make for a person go to work for Colonel Sanders, then declare that they are a vegetarian and refuse to sell chicken – and still keep their job?

Conservative majorities and conservative leaders have shown in the past that they do not want to encourage birth control, and indeed in many cases would eliminate it altogether. The future of domestic and international family planning programs, and therefore the fate of many women who may need birth control but cannot afford it, is in the hands of voters.

Policies that influence women's choices and options are most definitely on the table in '08, in both state and federal elections.

Questions for candidates:

Do you believe in an individual's right to access to birth control without interference from the government?

Do you support providing birth control for poor women through Medicaid without co-pays, which are not affordable for most poor women?

Do you support U.S. aid to international family planning programs?

Do you believe pharmacists should be able to refuse to fill legal prescriptions for any drug the pharmacy normally carries?

Do you think insurance companies should be required to provide coverage for birth control prescriptions?

If an insurance company provides coverage for Viagra-type drugs, should that company also be required to cover birth control prescriptions?

Access to Abortion

"For today, the women of this Nation still retain the liberty to control their destinies. But the signs are evident and very ominous, and a chill wind blows."   —Justice Harry Blackmun, 1989 in the *Webster v. Reproductive Health Services* Supreme Court decision opening the way for state restrictions on abortion.

Some people believe that those who advocate for a woman's right to make her own reproductive choices are pushing "abortion on demand" on women. This is not the case. The so-called "abortion wars" are about a woman's right to control her own body and her medical privacy, not about the particular choices she makes in doing it.

Abortion rights advocates want women to be able to choose abortion, or choose to carry a pregnancy to term, without the interference of the government. They also believe that legal abortion should be available to women in other countries, because where abortion is outlawed, death rates from self-induced and illegal abortions are high – just as they once were in the United States.

Contrary to rhetoric from the anti-choice right wing, abortion rights advocates do not endorse abortion as a method of birth control. While many women would never make the choice to have an abortion, the abortion rights movement is about preserving their rights as autonomous human beings as well.

Abortion was legal in the United States from the time the earliest settlers arrived. At the time the Constitution was adopted, abortions before "quickening" were openly advertised and commonly performed. States began to criminalize abortion in the 1800s, and by 1910 all but one state had criminalized abortion except where necessary, in a doctor's judgment, to save the woman's life.

The impetus for outlawing abortion was threefold. Some feared that newly arriving immigrants had birth rates higher than native-born white women, so outlawing abortion would up the birth rate of these women, and therefore stave off "race suicide." Anti-abortion legislation was also part of a backlash to the growing movements for suffrage and birth control--an effort to control women and confine them to their traditional childbearing role.

Finally, the medical profession wanted more control over women's health.[132] Abortion was often performed by "untrained" practitioners, including midwives, apothecaries, and homeopaths, thus competing with physicians for patient dollars.

The best way for medical doctors to accomplish their goal was to eliminate one of the principle procedures that kept these competitors in business. Rather than openly admitting to such motivations, the newly formed American Medical Association (AMA) argued that abortion was both immoral and dangerous.[133]

Since very few abortions could be certified as necessary to save a woman's life, women were forced into the back alleys. Criminalizing the procedure did not reduce the numbers of women who sought abortions. Although accurate records were not kept, it is known that between the 1880s and 1973, many thousands of women were harmed as a result of illegal abortion.

In the years before the Supreme Court legalized the procedure, the estimates of illegal abortions ranged as high as 1.2 million per year. Hospital emergency rooms treated thousands of women, many of whom died, and many suffered lasting health effects.[134]

Beginning in the 1960s with the women's liberation movement, one-third of the states liberalized or repealed their criminal abortion laws. The right to an abortion for all women in the U.S. was gained in 1973, when the Supreme Court struck down the remaining restrictive state laws with its ruling in *Roe v. Wade*.

The ruling said that Americans' right to privacy included the right of a woman to decide whether to have children, and the right of a woman and her doctor to make that decision without interference from the state. It was not a ruling that granted wholesale "abortion on demand" to women.

Roe's trimester-based analysis generally prohibited regulation of abortions in the first three months, allowed regulation for protecting the health of the mother in the second three months, and allowed complete abortion bans after six months, the approximate time a fetus becomes viable (able to survive on its own outside the womb).

After the ruling, the anti-choice forces mobilized, and they continue to work to prevent state funding for the procedure for poor women, to eliminate abortion counseling at home and in other countries through withholding U.S. family planning funds, and to mount campaigns and lawsuits to make abortion very difficult to obtain.

Many also picket abortion clinics. Some clinics have been bombed or burned to the ground. Doctors are routinely targeted for harassment, and some have been murdered.

Since President Bush took office, there have been 2570 violent incidents nationwide against abortion clinics, including burning one in Albuquerque, N.M. in December, 2007. There have been 72 outright blockades of clinics. Though such blockades are against federal law, only 3 incidents have resulted in arrest.[135]

Violence, harassment, disruption, and blockades are actions that amount to domestic terrorism against the clinics, doctors, and the women who seek their services.

Anti-choice forces have also mounted concentrated legal attacks, passing restrictive state laws. Abortion law has become much narrower since *Roe*, including restricting pre-viability procedures, mandatory waiting periods, biased counseling, and parental and judicial involvement.

Some legal entities, including the U.S. Justice Department under President Bush and the Kansas Attorney General, have tried to force hospitals to release women's private medical records, saying they're needed to determine if a crime has been committed.[136]

A number of cases have been litigated all the way to the Supreme Court. The first outright federal abortion ban, prohibiting one type of procedure unless the life (but explicitly excluding the health) of the woman is at stake, was upheld in 2007. The result of this is that while abortion remains legal in the U.S., it is increasing harder to obtain. Not only are the above restrictions in place in many states, but clinics have shut down due to harassment.

Eighty eight percent of counties in the U.S. have no identifiable abortion provider, and the number rises to 97% in rural counties. That means one in four women have to travel over 50 miles, and 8% travel 100 miles or more.[137] With mandatory waiting periods and the inability of many women to miss work, this puts abortion out of reach.

A Timeline of Reproductive Rights[*]

1821: Connecticut passes the first law in the United States barring abortions after "quickening."

1860: Twenty states have laws limiting abortion.

1965: *Griswold v. Connecticut* Supreme Court decision strikes down a state law that prohibited giving married people information, instruction, or medical advice on contraception.

1967: Colorado is the first state to liberalize its abortion laws.

1970: Alaska, Hawaii, New York, and Washington liberalize abortion laws, making abortion available at the request of a woman and her doctor.

1972: *Eisenstadt v. Baird* Supreme Court decision establishes the right of unmarried people to use contraceptives.

---

[*]Timeline from the National Abortion Federation, Washington, D.C., www.prochoice.org

1973: *Roe v. Wade* Supreme Court decision strikes down state laws that made abortion illegal.

1976: Congress adopts the first Hyde Amendment barring the use of federal Medicaid funds to provide abortions to low-income women.

1977: A revised Hyde Amendment is passed allowing states to deny Medicaid funding except in cases of rape, incest, or "severe and long-lasting" damage to the woman's physical health.

1991: *Rust v. Sullivan* upholds the constitutionality of the 1988 "gag rule" which prohibits doctors and counselors at clinics receiving federal funding from providing their patients with information about and referrals for abortion.

1992: *Planned Parenthood of Southeastern Pennsylvania v. Casey* reaffirms the "core" holdings of *Roe* that women have a right to abortion before fetal viability, but allows states to restrict abortion access so long as these restrictions do not impose an "undue burden" on women seeking abortions.

1994: Freedom of Access to Clinic Entrances (FACE) Act passes Congress by a large majority in response to the murder of Dr. David Gunn. The FACE Act forbids the use of "force, threat of force or physical obstruction" to prevent someone from providing or receiving reproductive health services. The law also provides for both criminal and civil penalties for those who break the law.

2000: *Stenberg v. Carhart* (Carhart I) rules that the Nebraska statute banning so-called "partial-birth abortion" is unconstitutional for two independent reasons: the statute lacks the necessary exception for preserving the health of the woman, and the definition of the targeted procedures is so broad as to prohibit abortions in the second trimester, thereby being an "undue burden" on women. This effectively invalidates 29 of 31 similar statewide bans.

2000: Food and Drug Administration approves mifepristone (RU-486) as an option in abortion care for very early pregnancy.

2003: A federal ban on one type of abortion procedure is passed by Congress and signed into law by President Bush. The National Abortion Federation immediately challenges the law in court and is successful in blocking enforcement of the law for its members. Two other legal challenges (Carhart II, see below) were also mounted.

2004: *National Abortion Federation v. Gonzales*. NAF wins lawsuit against the federal abortion ban. The Bush Justice Department appeals rulings by three trial courts against the ban to the U.S. Supreme Court. The case remains on hold pending the outcome of Carhart II.

2006: *Ayotte v. Planned Parenthood of Northern New England*, challenged a New Hampshire's law requiring doctors to delay a teenager's abortion until 48 hours after a parent was notified, but lacking a medical emergency exception to protect a pregnant teenager's health. In a unanimous decision, the Court reiterated its long-standing principle that abortion restrictions must include protections for women's health.[138]

2007: *Gonzales v. Carhart* and *Gonzales v. Planned Parenthood Federation of America*, (Carhart II) In a 5-4 decision, the new Roberts Court upheld the federal abortion ban, undermining a core principle of *Roe v. Wade*: that women's health must remain paramount, and essentially overturning its decision in *Stenberg v. Carhart* (Carhart I), issued only seven years earlier.

Writing for the majority, Justice Kennedy evoked antiquated notions of women's place in society and called into question their decision-making ability, said lawmakers could overrule a doctor's medical judgment, and that the "state's interest in promoting respect for human life at all stages in the pregnancy" could out-weigh a woman's interest in protecting her health.[139]

It is uncertain whether *Roe v. Wade* will be overturned outright in the next few years, but it is looking increasingly likely with the new hard-core conservative Supreme Court majority against abortion rights.

Those who think abortion will still be legal, only "just go back to the states," as many like to say, need to think again. As of December 2007, 43 states had laws on the books that will restrict the legal status of abortion or outlaw it altogether (commonly called trigger laws) when *Roe* is overturned.[140]

And don't fall for the line that these are "old" pre-*Roe* laws that will never be enforced – only 13 fall into that category, and there is certainly no guarantee that they won't stand up. In fact, anti-choice state legisla-tors in many states can be expected to "stand guard" to see that these laws are not overturned.

Chillingly, some states rushed to pass new trigger bans in 2007, in anticipation of a *Roe* overturn, right after the Carhart II decision (see timeline above).

Even if state legislatures are not inclined to pass restrictive laws, anti-choice activists have shown they will use state ballot initiatives to outlaw or restrict abortion. Ballot measures are proposed state laws that must be approved or rejected directly by voters within states. They can be placed on the ballot by legislatures, citizen petitions or other methods, and are most often held in conjunction with general elections.

In California and Oregon, abortion-restriction ballot measures pushed by anti-choice forces were defeated by voters in 2006. Conversely, the women's rights movement was forced to use the initiative process in South Dakota to repeal an abortion ban, which included no exceptions for a victim of rape or incest or if a woman's health is endangered, that had been passed by the legislature and signed by the governor. Had the law not been repealed, proponents of the ban had envisioned it as a test case for outright repeal of *Roe* in subsequent court challenges.

It is daunting to say the least that the pro-choice movement will have to fight abortion bans state by state, year after year if there are no federal protections. State ballot initiatives are already planned for 2008.

In Colorado, anti-abortion activists are working for an initiative that extends constitutional protections to fertilized eggs by defining them as persons. If passed, the initiative would also threaten the contraceptives used by millions of women, including the IUD and emergency contraceptives.

A proposed Missouri ballot initiative would require doctors to investigate each patient's background and lifestyle before providing abortion services.[141]

The right to reproductive choice and medical privacy is the single biggest issue at stake for women's lives and health in the '08 election and beyond. It is not only relevant to young women who may be faced with the abortion decision, but to all women who value their autonomy and privacy.

Because it is both a federal and state issue and bans are looming at both levels, it is particularly important to confront candidates at all levels as to their views and intentions.

Questions for candidates:

Do you support a woman's right to abortion as embodied in *Roe. v. Wade?*

Do you support or oppose appointments to the Supreme Court of people who would overturn *Roe v. Wade?*

Do you support any restrictions on the right to choose? If yes, which ones?

If *Roe v. Wade* is overturned, would you support a federal Freedom of Choice Act guaranteeing a woman's right to privacy in medical decisions, including whether or not to have an abortion?

TEN

Your Life: Health Care

An increasingly burdensome economic problem for women and their families is the availability and cost of health care. In a 2006 election poll women rated health care second only to the war in importance. Forty six percent of women ranked health care their highest priority (54% said the war).

In contrast, only 33% of men said health care was their main concern – a 13 point gender gap. Perhaps this is because more men have insurance coverage through their employers.

Even so, sixty four percent of men and women alike tell pollsters that health insurance companies refusing to pay for medical treatments, even when doctors say they are necessary, is a serious problem.[142]

The Insurance Problem

By far the most common health coverage in the United States is privately purchased from for-profit insurance companies, by employers and individuals. Every year $1.9 trillion is spent in the U.S. on care -- some $6,280 for every woman, child, and man in the country.

Health care expenditures are 16 percent of the U.S. economy, well above the figure for any other industrialized country. Even so, when we compare health outcomes -- measurements such as infant mortality or life expectancy-- the U.S. trails behind these nations.[143] Virtually every country in Europe has universal health care, as do Australia, Canada, and Japan.

The average cost of health insurance for an American family now exceeds the yearly income of a minimum wage worker – and the majority of minimum wage workers are adult women. That's probably a big reason why 47 million people in the U.S. have no health insurance, including almost one in five women.

The numbers are miserable when broken down by race: 22% of African American women go without insurance, 36% of Native American women, and a whopping 38% of Hispanic women are not covered.[144] Over 15% of women have no first trimester pre-natal care.[145]

Far too many children in our country are going without health insurance as well. According to the government's own figures, one in 10 U.S. children is uninsured, and one in 20 has no usual source of health care. About 1.8 million kids have been unable to see a doctor because the family cannot afford it, and 12% of the uninsured have not seen a doctor in over 2 years (some have *never* seen a doctor).

Not surprisingly, children in single mother families are the most likely to be unable to get health care when they need it.[146] Yet when Congress tried to expand the number of kids covered under the State Children's Health Insurance Program 2007 (SCHIP), President Bush vetoed it twice.

The Drug Cost Problem

Drug prices are another health concern, particularly for women. Women between the ages of 15 and 44 spend 68 % more on out-of-pocket health costs than do men, much of it on contraception. For young women, birth control is the single largest outlay, since insurance companies often refuse to cover contraceptive pills (even though many cover Viagra).

The American College Health Association reports that the deficit-reduction package signed by President Bush in 2006 caused contraceptive prices to soaring at college campuses across the country. According to college health officials, the hikes are five to sixfold, and have resulted in many college women stopping birth control altogether.[147]

At the same time, AARP reports that drug prices for drugs commonly used by older adults have been rising at twice the rate of inflation.[148] For older women on fixed incomes, higher drug prices can cause cut-backs on needed drugs, or hard choices between drugs and food or heat.

Because soaring drug prices can disproportionately affect women, another issue voters should attend to is importation of drugs from other countries such as Canada, where the same drugs are cheaper. Prices for brand-name drugs in the U.S. are among the highest in the world, but it is currently illegal for private citizens to import drugs from other countries. In many other industrialized nations, prices are lower because they are either controlled or partially controlled by government regulation.

Members of Congress who are trying to legalize the safe importation of drugs believe allowing imports would drive down the price of U.S. brand-name drugs. One example given is the cholesterol drug Lipitor, which costs about twice as much here as it does in Canada.[149]

For older women, the inability of the Medicare system to bargain with big pharmaceutical companies for better drug prices keeps prices high. Congress prohibited such bargaining when it passed the Medicare drug benefit in 2003.

Solutions

Experts agree that there is no silver bullet when it comes to fixing our health care system. Major factors include lack of technology for sharing information between hospitals, doctors, and other providers, use of emergency rooms as primary care by the uninsured, and not enough emphasis on prevention. By some estimates, chronic diseases such as diabetes cost the economy $1 trillion annually, much of it for treatment instead of prevention.[150]

Other budget busters are drug costs, overuse of expensive tests, not enough coordinated care, and over-reliance on specialists. Regardless, virtually no one on either side of the political spectrum denies that there is a problem we must solve as a country.

Approaches to the solution vary widely, however. In general, Democratic candidates emphasize "universal coverage" – meaning everyone would have health insurance. Means of achieving the goal vary, but it's fair to say most would preserve the present role of insurance companies. Some would mandate that people buy health insurance, much like auto insurance. Others mandate only that parents get insurance for their kids.

Methods of paying the bill also vary, but most schemes involve a partnership between employers, workers, and the government, with more help for people who are too poor to afford coverage at all (similar to the present Medicaid system). A few advocate "Medicare for All," which would mean a single payer system (see below), eliminating the control of for-profit insurance companies over our health care system.

Republicans generally believe the medical system should be "market based," rely on "individual responsibility," and not involve the government at all. Many refer to government involvement as "socialized medicine." (It is unclear whether they believe public schools are "socialized education," and if so, whether that is bad for U.S. kids.)

The schemes that rely on the market involve further deregulation of the insurance industry, and leaving health care solutions up to the states "instead of "relying on a one-size-fits-all, government-run system."[151]

If you are confused, you're not alone. But if voters are to be actively engaged in the dialogue from candidates and parties about health care, they need to know what the terms being bandied about actually mean, and not rely on rhetoric that is often times not accurate.

Rhetoric vs. Reality

"Universal coverage" means just that – everyone would have health insurance. Some would have it through employers, the very poor through government-subsidized programs, and some through privately purchased plans that might be subsidized by the government, depending on income.

Universal coverage does *not* mean the government would provide health care as a "welfare" or "entitlement" benefit to everyone, regardless of income or employment status. If the universal coverage currently advocated by most candidates was not achieved through a single payer system, the for-profit insurance industry would remain in place and would play a primary role in achieving universal coverage.

Choice of doctors and hospitals under universal coverage would remain much as it is now – controlled by the type of plan the individual is covered under and in no small part dictated by insurance companies. In some scenarios, insurance companies would be required to cover pre-existing conditions, stopping the practice of "cherry-picking" only the healthiest patients for inclusion in their plans.

"Single payer" means a system of health care characterized by universal and comprehensive coverage, and the government would be the insurer issuing the payments. Everyone's health care would be paid for out of one publicly administered trust fund (funded by taxes on both individuals and business) which would replace our current multi-payer system. Premiums to insurance companies would be eliminated.

While *single payer eliminates the role of insurance companies and the premiums paid to them,* the government would not be the primary *provider* of health care. It would just the primary *payer.* There would still be freedom to choose doctors and other health care professionals, facilities, and services. Doctors would remain in private practice and be paid on a fee-for-service basis from government funds. The government would not own or manage their medical practices or hospitals.

Single payer is the traditional Medicare model (not the new Medicare Advantage, which is an insurance-company-controlled HMO that does limit choice). Other countries with single payer include Canada, Australia, and Japan.

Proponents of single payer systems, including many physicians and groups such as Physicians for a National Health Program (http://www.pnhp.org), cite huge savings from eliminating insurance companies. These companies, as the "middle man" in health coverage, spend billions on non-health care related expenses such as advertising and lobbying in Washington.

In January 2008, physicians in Massachusetts, where there is a system that mandates universal coverage through the use of insurance companies, issued an open letter to the country that reads in part:

> Although we wish that the current reform could secure health insurance for all, its failings reinforce our conviction that only a single payer program can assure patients the care they need ... While patients, the state and safety net providers struggle, private insurers have prospered under the new law, and the costs of bureaucracy have risen ... All of

the major insurers in our state continue to charge overhead costs five times higher than Medicare and eleven-fold higher than Canada's single payer system ... A single payer program could save Massachusetts more than $9 billion annually on health care bureaucracy, making universal coverage affordable.[152]

Single-payer health care is distinct and different from "socialized medicine," a system of health care in which the government owns health facilities, and health personnel work for the government and draw their salaries from the government. This is the model used in the U.S. Veterans Administration and the armed services, where the government owns the medical facilities and medical professionals are government employees.

International examples of socialized medicine can be found in Great Britain and Spain.[153] Red-hot rhetoric notwithstanding, none of the candidates, nor either political party, presently advocates socialized medicine in the United States.

The outcome of the 2008 election will not only determine the direction of the debate over the next four years, but also the kinds of changes in our health care system that are possible.

Questions for candidates:

Do you support universal health coverage?

Would you require insurance companies to cover everyone?

If you support universal health coverage, what kind of program would you put in place – keep insurance companies or go to single-payer? How would you pay for it?

What do you propose to do about increasing costs and decreasing benefits in insurance coverage?

Do you think that insurance companies such as Blue Cross/Blue Shield, which awarded its chairman a $16.4 million retirement bonus and pays him a $3 million salary,[154] are making excess profits?

Do you favor safe importation of drugs from other countries such as Canada, where the same drugs can cost half as much as in the U.S.? Do you propose *other* fixes for high drug costs? What are they?

Do you think insurance companies that cover Viagra-type drugs should also be required to cover birth control prescriptions?

Would you, or have you, sponsored a bill to decrease the cost of birth control to college students?

Publicly Funded Medical Insurance Programs
In the U.S.

Medicare

While most health insurance in the U.S. is provided through private employer or personal funds, we have a few significant publicly funded medical insurance programs that are important to voters. The largest is Medicare, which is for people 65 and up and certain disabled people under 65. Though most of Medicare is paid for by the federal government, it requires a monthly premium from recipients.

Medicare is especially important to women, because they outlive men and will need health care coverage for a longer period of their lives. Women are also less likely to have private pensions that cover some medical needs like drugs, or provide supplemental coverage.

Medicare (Part A) covers only hospitalization or brief follow up care in a nursing facility. The vast majority of recipients meet eligibility requirements that do not require a payment for Part A.

But Part A does not cover doctor visits, diagnostic tests, medical equipment and the like. So most recipients also buy a supplemental Medicare policy (Part B) to cover these shortfalls, and a third private supplemental policy (generally dubbed Medigap) to cover everything the first two do not, such as deductibles.

People insured under these traditional Medicare plans have complete control over their choice of doctors, hospitals, and specialists, though a very few facilities and doctors do not take Medicare.

As noted above, Medicare is a single-payer system – and the government is that payer. That means people on Medicare do not have to file claims or hassle with insurance companies.

In 2008, Medicare Part B cost $96.40 per month (with high income recipients paying slightly more). A mid-priced supplemental Medigap policy (e.g one that would cover deductibles but not treatment in a foreign country) cost about $125 per month, depending on age and state of residence.

Medicare premiums are rising rapidly, as are the costs of Medigap policies which must be purchased from private insurance companies. Part B premiums have nearly doubled in the past five years. This is particularly important for older women, because their retirement incomes are lower than those of men, and women are less likely to get help with Medigap from former employers.

Though managed care (HMO-type) programs have been available to enrollees under Medicare since 1997, they have been greatly expanded since 2006 when the old plans were renamed Medicare Advantage and incentives were created for traditional HMOs to participate.

Medicare Advantage plans are required to offer drug coverage under Part D (below) and basic Medicare services. Beyond that, the government does not regulate them. That means that they can impose traditional managed care restrictions such as limiting choice of doctors and hospitals, and denying coverage for services or treatments (they also get to rule on any appeals you make when they deny coverage). Medicare sends them a check every month on the patient's behalf, but the plans are free to set premiums and co-pays at any level they like.[155]

The Congressional Budget Office estimates that the federal government spends about 12% more on Medicare Advantage (HMO) patients than on regular Medicare enrollees. There have been many reported abuses in the selling of Medicare Advantage programs by insurance companies, including agents telling seniors they are "from Medicare," and the use of very high pressure sales tactics.

It has gotten so bad that state insurance commissioners want to prosecute the companies — but federal law does not allow states to pursue Medicare Advantage plans for fraud, as they can in other insurance markets.[156] Critics in Congress and such organizations as the American Medical Association and AARP say the plans are nothing more than a subsidy for private insurers – at a time when the Bush administration proposes cutting physician fees for traditional Medicare enrollees.

Eliminating subsidies to Medicare Advantage programs would save the government more than $50 billion over five years, and $150 billion over ten years.[157] Congress proposed cutting Medicare Advantage overpayments in 2007, but relented after a threatened Bush veto.

Many candidates will say Medicare is bankrupting the country, and we should cut back on it or start means-testing recipients. If Medicare is eliminated or even significantly curtailed, families will have to take up the slack. It is very important for women, and female voters must ask the right questions before casting their ballots.

Questions for candidates:

> Do you favor cutting fees that doctors get for treating patients enrolled in traditional Medicare?

> Do you favor cutting services under traditional Medicare?

> Do you think Medicare Advantage HMO programs should be paid more per patient than those in traditional Medicare, even though the plans can dictate choice of doctors, deny treatments and raise co-pays and premiums at will?

> How would you control fraud and abuse by insurance companies in the selling of Medicare Advantage programs to seniors?

Drug Coverage Under Medicare

In 2003 Congress passed the first drug coverage program under Medicare; it became operative in 2006. Part of the Medicare Prescription Drug, Improvement, and Modernization Act, it is called Medicare Part D. There are two basic plans: stand-alone Prescription Drug Plans (PDPs) or prescription drug coverage under Medicare Advantage (HMO) plans (above). Both types are approved and regulated very loosely by the Medicare program, but are actually designed and administered by private health insurance companies.

Unlike Original Medicare (Part A and B), and Medigap policies, Part D coverage is not standardized. Insurance companies choose which drugs (or even classes of drugs) they wish to cover, at what level (or tier) they wish to cover it, and are free to choose not to cover some drugs at all. Plans are also free to change the drugs they cover from year to year, and to change co-pays and premiums.

Part D has come under much criticism from advocacy organizations, senior citizens, and members of Congress – though they're the ones that passed it. There are several serious problems.

- The legislation creating the plan *prohibits the federal government from negotiating with drug companies for the lowest drug prices*. Studies have shown that prices charged by Medicare Part D drug plans are 46% higher than those paid by the Veterans' Administration which does negotiate with the pharmaceutical companies.[158]

- There is a *coverage gap, known as the"donut hole,"* which kicks in after drug costs reach $2,510 in a given year and continues until they reach $4,050, even though seniors must continue to pay Part D monthly premiums. This means many people pay 100% of their drug costs for part of the year, plus premiums. For the average senior, this is about 3 ½ months, over one quarter of the year.[159]

    In 2005 Senator Lautenberg (D-NJ) offered an amendment to the Prescription Drug Plan that would have required Medicare beneficiaries to sign a disclaimer that they understood, in plain English, the coverage gap in their plan before they could enroll in it. The amendment was defeated 43-56 with every single Republican in the Senate in opposition.

- Plans are not standardized and are extremely confusing. Companies can *change the drugs covered or drop drugs from coverage altogether*, meaning people must shop all over again each year for a plan that covers the drugs they take. Plans can also raise the co-pays and premiums at will, and most have done so in great leaps.[160]

- There are also *problems for low income people* who previously had coverage under Social Security Supplemental Security Income, where their prescription costs were paid by Medicaid. Part D replaced that Medicaid coverage, and most of these people were automatically assigned to a Part D plan without any evaluation of their necessary prescriptions. Co-pays were instituted as well.

Questions for Candidates:

Do you favor closing the "donut hole" in Medicare Part D drug coverage?

Do you favor allowing Medicare to negotiate prices with drug companies?

Do you favor standardizing drug plans the same way Medigap policies are standardized?

Medicaid

Medicaid is a state administered health insurance program for the poor that is paid for in large part by the federal government through block grants (lump sum payments given to the states to spend under their state rules.)

Almost 60% of those enrolled in Medicaid are female[161] – women have lower incomes overall and are also the most frequent custodial parents of children who are on Medicaid.

Even though states have leeway in crafting their Medicaid programs, they must comply with federal standards to get the federal government's money. Nevertheless, until 2007, states were generally free to set their own eligibility criteria for recipients. (For a discussion of how recent Medicaid rule changes have affected women and family planning, see pp. 90-91.)

In December 2007, the Bush administration announced that it was imposing more restrictions on the states' ability to expand Medicaid eligibility criteria to provide health insurance to more low income families, "in an effort to prevent them from offering coverage to families of modest incomes who may have access to private health insurance."[162] States had wanted to cover families of four making less than $60 thousand per year, instead of $50 thousand, the current standard.

A family spends about one-third of its income on food, another one-third on housing, leaving only one-third ($16 thousand under the current standard) to cover everything else, including health insurance. In 2007, insurance coverage for families averaged

$12,106, up 105% since 2000.[163] If a family paid that premium, it would leave only $333 per month to pay for such basics as transportation, school expenses, and clothing, not to mention emergencies.

Questions for candidates:

> Do you support allowing states to expand Medicaid eligibility?

> What would you do for families that are just over Medicaid cutoffs, but don't make enough to buy insurance?

State Children's Health Insurance Program (SCHIP)

The State Children's Health Insurance Program is a government funded program to provide health insurance for low-income children who are not covered under Medicaid.

SCHIP was created in 1997 to cover kids in families with too much income to qualify for Medicaid, but without enough to afford private insurance. The program was passed by a Republican Congress and signed by a Democratic president.

According to the Commonwealth Fund, a private foundation working for better health care, "the program represents a fine balance, designed to maintain equilibrium between states and the federal government, as well as between political conservatives and liberals."[164]

Like Medicaid, states have flexibility in designing benefits for SCHIP, with the federal government paying an average of 70% of the cost and the states 30%. But also like Medicaid, the states must comply with federal requirements to get federal money.

In the original SCHIP bill, children in families making 200% of the poverty line could be covered. When the program came up for reauthorization in 2007, Democrats in Congress tried to raise the level to 300% of poverty. (The poverty line is $21,200 for a family of four.)

President Bush vetoed the bill, saying it would be "an incremental step toward the goal of government-run health care." (His spokeswoman had charged the week before that it would be "socialized-type medicine.") Both statements were inaccurate, as the program would be administered by private insurers and delivered by private nurses and doctors.[165] Congress was unable to override the veto, leaving the standard for eligibility at 1997 levels.

Questions for candidates:

Do you favor covering more low income families under Medicaid and SCHIP?

How much money do you think a family of four should be able to make and qualify for health insurance under Medicaid? Under SCHIP?

Do you think most families who make a few thousand dollars more than this can realistically buy health insurance on their own?

Do you know how much private insurance costs per year for a family of four?

Veteran's Administration Health Care

The Veterans Administration (VA), has traditionally provided VA care to all veterans, with copays for those veterans considered to be "non-poor" (generally those making $30,000 and higher).

In January 2003, however, the Bush administration ordered a halt to the enrollment of "non-poor" veterans, citing not enough capacity. As a result, according to a Harvard Medical School study, millions of vets and their family members cannot afford health insurance and go without needed medical care. Others are unable to obtain VA care due to waiting lists at some VA facilities, unaffordable copayments for VA specialty care, or the lack of VA facilities in their communities.[166]

Estimates of veterans without health coverage are now at 1.8 million. While women are a small percentage of veterans, they are especially vulnerable to cuts because of their lower incomes and longer lifetime needs for health care.

Questions for candidates:

Do you believe our veterans should have access to VA health care regardless of income?

Some have suggested a "heroes health card" for veterans, allowing them to get health care at any facility they choose, not just VA hospitals. Do you support this idea?

ELEVEN

Your Money: Social Security

Social Security is one of the largest entitlement programs provided by the federal government. It is always an election year issue, because the money outlays are huge, because the population is aging, and because candidates like to use "the Social Security crisis" as a fear-mongering tactic or a way to promote schemes that will undermine the program, with the ultimate goal of eliminating it altogether.

Before we get to a discussion of "fixes" candidates and lawmakers propose, a few quick facts about Social Security are in order.

- Social Security does *not* face an immediate crisis, although there is a significant, but man-ageable, long-term financing problem.

- Social Security is in no danger of "running out of money." The Social Security Trust Fund is currently running a surplus. According to the Congressional Budget Office, with *no changes at all* Social Security can pay full benefits through 2052, and 80% of promised benefits after that.[167]

- Social Security is not draining the economy. The program consumes a smaller share of the gross domestic product today that it did when Ronald Reagan was elected in 1980.[168]

– Between 2008 and 2030 the baby boomers will cause a slight increase in Social Security outlays, after which costs will even out and resume a gradual and manageable growth rate.[169]

Now let's look at a few quick facts about Social Security and its largest group of beneficiaries – women:

- Women represent 57 percent of all Social Security beneficiaries age 62 and older and approximately 70 percent of beneficiaries age 85 and older.[170] In addition to providing benefits to retired female workers, Social Security provides dependent benefits to spouses, divorced spouses, elderly widows, and widows with young children.
- For both women and men 65 and older, Social Security is the largest source of income compared with other sources including earnings, private pensions, and income from assets such as savings accounts.[171]
- In 2006, 43.4 percent of all elderly unmarried females receiving Social Security benefits relied on Social Security for 90 percent or more of their income.[172]
- The average annual Social Security income received by women 65 years and older in 2006 was 25% less than that of men – $10,303, compared to $13,644.[173]

- Social Security is progressive – meaning it provides more generous benefits to lower lifetime earners for the amount of taxes paid in when compared to higher earners. Because women are still the lowest earners as a group, even when working full time and year round, they benefit from this distribution toward lower earners.
- Without Social Security, more than two thirds of elderly women would live in poverty.[174]

No one disputes that long-term financing for Social Security is something we must attend to as a nation, since it could eventually pay out more than it takes in if unless some adjustments are made.

Candidates and parties propose various solutions, and present a variety of scare tactic arguments about bankruptcy of the system or even bankruptcy of the country if nothing is done.

In fact, according to experts including the director of the Congressional Budget Office, threats to the economy from health care costs are far more significant than any impact from Social Security or retirement of the baby boomers.[175]

Fixing the Shortfall

Setting aside doomsday scenarios, both the government and a number of respected think tanks have put forth ways to close the gap between what Social Security takes in and what it will eventually have to pay out (called the "solvency target").

- For 2008 earnings subject to the Social Security payroll tax (called "the cap") are $102,000 per worker per year. Anything over that is not taxed, meaning the very highest earners, including billionaires and CEOs garnering multi-million dollar salaries, pay nothing on their incomes over $102,000. According to the government's own figures, eliminating the cap would virtually eliminate the projected 75-year funding shortfall.[176] And, it would make the Social Security tax much fairer.

- Investing 15% of the Social Security Trust fund in stocks, instead of the Treasury Bills currently used, would eliminate 13% of the shortfall.[177] Investing 40% would eliminate almost half of it.[178] This is an approach used by many state pension funds. (Note: this is *not* the same thing as privatizing Social Security – see below.)

- Increasing the payroll tax less than 1 percentage point each for employers and employee contributions would eliminate 50% of the shortfall.[179]

Obviously the first alternative is the easiest, and by far the fairest. Yet the Bush administration has repeatedly insisted that the only way to "save" Social Security is by cutting benefits, privatizing the system, or both.

Privatizing Social Security means allowing individuals to divert part or all of the money they now put in Social Security into private accounts. Experts agree that privatization is not a solution, and would in fact make the projected shortfall in Social Security much worse.[180]

Cutting benefits would have a disproportionately negative impact on women and so would privatization, which is opposed by AARP as well as all of the major U.S. women's groups.[181]

The scheme is particularly dangerous for women for a number of reasons. Women live longer, and cannot outlive Social Security benefits, which are guaranteed for life. Investments are risky and can be wiped out completely in economic downturns. Women would have smaller amounts to invest, resulting in smaller payouts that might not last a lifetime.

Most importantly, Social Security provides benefits to widows and divorced spouses. There is no guarantee that a spouse would leave a private account to his or her widow, and it is almost certain such accounts would not be left to an ex-spouse. There is also no provision for division of private accounts in divorce.

Positive Social Security Changes for Women[*]

In addition to strengthening the long-term outlook for Social Security, we need to be thinking of ways that

---

[*]Social Security is gender neutral, meaning benefits of spouses, divorced individuals, and widows are available to both women and men on an equal basis. But since women are still by far the lower earners, these proposed improvements would have a proportionately greater benefit to women.

the system can be strengthened and made more fair for women.

In 1999, the largest coalition of women's advocacy groups in the country convened a meeting to talk about how to do this. They came up with a number of recommendations, all of which could be paid for through adjustments such as those above.[182]

After almost a decade, some candidates and members of Congress are now talking about these changes, though they will need a push from women if any of them are to become reality.

> *Family service credit:* Currently those who drop out of the work force to care for children or elderly parents get a zero in the their Social Security account for each year spent care-giving. This brings down the level of benefits at retirement, because those "zero years" of earn-ings are averaged in. A family service credit would mean caregivers would be given credit – at the level of minimum wage – for years out of the workforce when children are under the age of six, or providing two "drop out" years when elderly parents need a full time caregiver.

> *Improve eligibility for divorced spouses:* Currently an ex-spouse can collect benefits based on a former spouse's higher earnings if they were married ten years. Improving the eligibility criteria would mean dropping this requirement to seven years, or a total of ten years of mar-riage and work history combined.

Improve widow(er)s benefit: Widows are the majority of the elderly poor, and their economic circumstances worsen as they age. Depending on their particular situation, widows currently collect half to two-thirds of the combined benefit when the primary earner dies. This benefit should be raised to 75% of the couple's joint benefit, to go no higher than the highest earner's maximum benefit.

Questions for candidates:

Do you support diverting part or all of Social Security contributions to private accounts?

Would you remove the cap on earnings taxed for Social Security so that the very rich pay their fair share? If not, why not?

Does your plan for strengthening Social Security involve benefit cuts?

Does your plan help those with lower lifetime earnings, usually meaning women?

Do you think we should strengthen benefits for widows, lower earning spouses, and divorced spouses? How?

Do you support giving some Social Security credit for years spend caring for children or elderly parents?

TWELVE

Your Life: Long-term Care

In the U.S., long-term care is treated as a private problem, unless you are among the poorest. Even then, there are few government resources. Medicare, the nation's medical insurance system for those over 65, does not pay for personal or custodial services or long-term care.

Medicaid, which provides health insurance for those with very low incomes and few if any savings or assets, will pay for nursing home or home-based care. But services and benefits depend on the state where you live, and generally assets must be "spent down" in order to qualify.

The Department of Veterans Affairs (VA) *may* provide long-term care for service-related disabilities or for certain eligible veterans (e.g. low income).[183]

Long-term Care in Other Countries

This puts the U.S. behind other developed nations in long-term care policy and practice. Long-term and elder care varies in other countries, but many provide some assistance regardless of income.

According to an article by Martin Tolchin in the *New York Times*, "In Canada, 8 of the 10 provinces now provide some form of long-term care coverage for all citizens. The Netherlands provides long-term nursing home care for the entire population.

Japan offers two kinds of long-term care. There are geriatric hospitals that resemble American nursing homes, for those who need skilled medical care, and for which the Government pays the entire bill for those 70 years old and above.[184]

A Woman's Issue

Since the U.S. comes up short on both national policies and programs, long-term care is a problem that most families must solve on their own. And it is very much a women's issue.

The MetLife Mature Market Institute projects that half of U.S. adults will eventually need some kind of long-term care. Seventy-two percent of nursing home residents are female, and 90 percent of paid direct-care workers along with 61 percent of family caregivers are women.

Nationally, staff turnover in nursing homes averages 70 percent per year for aides and 50 percent for nurses, meaning patient care is uneven and unreliable.[185] Two thirds of U.S. nursing homes are owned by for-profit companies,[186] many of them corporate chains paying notoriously low wages, which are undoubtedly a major contributor to this turnover.

Purchasing Long-Term Care

Private long-term care insurance must be purchased on the open market from insurance companies, generally while the individual is still healthy – and preferably young – in order to be affordable. As a result, most long-term care services are either provided by unpaid caregivers (mostly female), or paid out-of-pocket. These expenses can approach $100,000 per year in some parts of the country. Obviously most families find this far out of reach.[187]

The cost of facilities and lack of community-based options means that many older Americans must rely on family and friends to provide care at home. Caregivers, particularly women and members of low-income families, are faced with tremendous stress.

Many get caught in a difficult spiral. They are forced to take time off from work, forgo promotions, and maybe even drop out of the workforce altogether to care for elderly relatives. Consequently, they work less and earn less, which reduces the Social Security and pension benefits they receive. And women, who generally live longer than men, must stretch their meager resources much further.

Needed: Changes in Public Policy

While we clearly do not have adequate long-term care supports, the need for long-term care could be reduced with changes in public policy. According to AARP, most older people and those with disabilities want to remain independent and get the assistance they need at home or in their communities, not in nursing homes. Providing care at home or in an assisted living facility can improve quality of life and provide better value for the dollars spent.

Many of the services elders need to stay in their own homes are not medical. Transportation, help with bill-paying, and help with shopping or daily self-care

are all services for which there is at present little or no support.

Providing support for these services, even funding volunteer networks, could go a long way toward keeping elders in their own homes longer, at the same time providing a higher quality of life than nursing home care that is expensive and oftentimes below par.

Questions for candidates:

> Are you satisfied with the fact that the U.S. lags far behind other developed nations when it comes to long-term care for the elderly?

> What would you do to ease the financial burden of long-term care on families?

> Do you think a federal or state program to provide affordable long-term care insurance is needed?

> Do you think Medicare should be expanded to include long-term care?

> How would you improve transportation options for seniors who can no longer drive?

> Should Medicaid and Medicare support non-medical services to keep seniors out of nursing homes longer?

> What would you do to improve the standards for nursing homes and insure that patients are cared for adequately?

Do you think the government should support pilot projects in liveable communities, with support services that keep seniors in their own homes longer, to see what works best? How would you do this?

THIRTEEN

Family Leave and Sick Leave

There are no federal or state laws guaranteeing sick leave for employees in the United States. Whether sick leave is granted is entirely up to employers (except in San Francisco, which passed a mandatory nine days for sick leave in 2006).

Paid Sick Leave

This puts us in stark contrast to other countries – 145 provide paid sick days for short or long-term illness, and more than 79 give 26 weeks of time off for illness, or provide leave until the worker recovers.[188]

Because there is no requirement for paid sick leave, nearly half of Americans have no benefit for self-care or to care for a family member. For the lowest earning families (bottom quartile), 79 percent have no paid sick leave. For families in the middle (next 2 quartiles), 46 and 38 percent, respectively, lack such leave. Even for families in the top fourth of the income bracket, 28 percent do without paid sick leave.

Even workers who are lucky enough to have paid sick leave are limited in how it can be used. A very high percentage of those with the benefit can use it only for personal illness; they can't use it to care for ill family members.[189]

State laws are not much help. Only a few states require employers that do offer the leave to broaden it to give workers greater flexibility in using their sick days (e.g. caring for sick kids).

Maine was the first state to pass a such a law in 2002; California, Connecticut, Hawaii, Minnesota, Washington and Wisconsin have since adopted similar measures.[190]

A bill called the Healthy Families Act was introduced in Congress in 2007. If it ever passes, it will require employers who employ 15 or more employees to provide minimum paid sick leave and employment benefits of: (1) seven days annually for those who work at least 30 hours per week; and (2) a prorated annual amount for part-timers working 20-29 hours a week (or who work between 1,000 and 1,500 hours per year). It would not affect workplaces that already have more generous sick leave policies.

So far, the bill, sponsored mostly by Democrats, has been referred to committees and has not been scheduled for hearings.

Pregnancy Leave

Like sick leave, there is no federal mandate that companies grant paid pregnancy leave. But there is a little more legal protection for pregnancy compared to sickness.

The Pregnancy Discrimination Act (passed in 1978) says if a woman is temporarily unable to perform her job due to pregnancy, the employer must treat her the same as any other temporarily disabled employee (e.g. someone who is injured or has had a heart attack).

So if the guys in the executive suites get leave time to recover from a coronary, the girls in the word processing department must be treated equally when it comes to pregnancy, since both would be considered a temporary disability. But if employers opt not to provide any paid time off for temporary disability, both workers are out of luck.

By way of comparison, out of 168 nations in a Harvard University study in 2004, 163 had some form of paid maternity leave, leaving the United States in the company of Lesotho, Papua New Guinea and Swaziland.[191]

If the U.S. ever gets paid family leave (see below), it will go a long way toward relieving some of the family and job stress associated with pregnancy and childbirth.

Family Leave

The United States has had *unpaid* family leave since 1993, when President Clinton signed the Family and Medical Leave Act (FMLA). It was the first major bill signed into law by the newly sworn-in president, after a long and bumpy ride to the Oval Office. FMLA was the result of eight years of Congressional debate, thirteen separate votes, and two vetoes by President George H. W. Bush.[192]

Basically, the FMLA grants 12 weeks of unpaid leave for workers (on the job at least a year) who work for a company with 50 or more employees. The leave can be used for serious health conditions of the employee, care of a seriously ill spouse, child, or parent, or for care, birth, or adoption of a child.

But the key word here is *unpaid*. Even for those whose employers are mandated to grant the benefit, many employees cannot afford to take it.

Once again, the U.S. lags behind other countries. Ninety eight of the 168 other countries that have guaranteed paid maternity leave offer 14 or more weeks off with pay, 66 provide paid paternal leave, and 37 ensure paid leave for illness of a child.[193]

There is no relief from the states. At this writing, only California has paid family leave, provided through the state unemployment insurance system. Senator Hillary Clinton has proposed giving grants to the states to study how to develop their own systems, but it is only a proposal at this stage.

In 2007 Senators Christopher Dodd and Ted Stevens introduced a bipartisan bill, the Family Leave Insurance Act, to provide 8 weeks of paid family leave. It is a comprehensive national plan that would be paid for by contributions from employers and employees on a cost sharing basis.

Employers and employees would pay into a giant insurance pool – much like Social Security – and the wage replacement would come from that pool when needed. Based on averages, the employer and employee would each pay each a little over $6.00 per month – more for higher earners, less for lower.

So don't let anyone tell you it would cause business to go bankrupt. The coverage would be mandated only for large employers (if they don't already have a better plan in place), but smaller ones could "opt in" for half price.

Nevertheless, business groups (and the candidates they support) generally do not favor such legislation.

Since women are still the primary caretakers in society and still make less than men overall, lack of paid leave can mean giving up a job altogether. And while an increasing number of men are also taking on caregiving obligations, men who ask for leave time are often denied or penalized because of stereotypes that caregiving is only "women's work."[194]

Women are in the workforce to stay, and it is in the national interest to craft a system whereby both women and men can take care of children and elderly parents when an emergency arises without losing their jobs or suffering setbacks at work.

The problems of work-family balance are not going to go away. Some lawmakers have recognized that by introducing legislation to help solve the problems, and candidates need to address them too. It is up to voters in '08 to pose the hard questions and determine whether a candidate supports family-friendly workplaces or not.

Questions for candidates:

Do you support paid sick leave for employees? Have you, or would you, co-sponsor one of the bills now in Congress to provide it?

Do you support both maternity and paternity leave for birth or adoption of a child?

Do you support *paid* family and medical leave? Have you, or would you, co-sponsor a bill to provide it?

Do you support a comprehensive national plan for paid sick days and paid family leave that does not depend on the state where an employee lives?

FOURTEEN

Child Care

As more and more women enter the work force and families cannot afford for one parent, or the only parent, to stay home, the need for quality, affordable child care increases. The overall labor force participation rate of mothers with children under 18 was 70.5% in 2005. Almost a third of all children live with only one parent, and about 81% of these children live with their mothers.[195]

Availability and Cost

The availability of affordable childcare can have a large impact on women's choices about work. Childcare is often prohibitively expensive: in 2002, the Organisation for Economic Co-operation and Development estimated that the cost of center-based care for two children in the U.S. could amount to as much as 37% of a single parent's income – a considerably larger portion than almost all other countries.[196]

Even for two-parent families of all income brackets, childcare tends to be the second-largest household expenditure after housing costs,[197] running from $5000 to $10,000 per child per year.[198]

While child care and pre-kindergarten are not the same thing, expansion of pre-k programs would help ease the child care crunch. Pre-k programs are administered by the states, and they vary widely, both in availability and funding.

According to the advocacy group Pre-K Now, state-funded pre-k programs currently serve less than 20 percent of three- and four-year-olds in the U.S. Only three states currently make pre-k available to all four-year-olds, and most have no state-funded pre-k program for three-year-olds. Ten states have no state-funded pre-k program at all.[199]

According to the *New York Times* using 2007 figures, the U.S. could have a year's worth of universal pre-school (half day for all three-year-olds, full day for all four-year-olds) for the cost of two months of the war.[200]

Child care is one of the most challenging problems facing families today, whether they are two- parent families or single mother families. U.S. parents pay almost all of their child care costs without state or federal assistance, amounting to a large portion of household income (25% for families below poverty level).[201] This is undoubtedly the main reason why enrollment in child care and early childhood education is lower in the U.S. than in other industrialized countries.[202]

Most families struggle with child care, regardless of whether their incomes are low, medium or high. That's because we have a hodge-podge of arrangements, and the availability of good care depends as much on where one lives as income.

Of course the higher one's income, the greater their ability to pay – if there is a decent program to pay *for*. Private in-home care by a nanny is almost exclusively limited to high income families, but even that does not guarantee the availability of a trustworthy and competent caregiver.

Wages for child care providers, whether in homes or in child care centers, are notoriously low – ranging from $7.60 per hour in Houston to $11.93 in Chicago, with most under $8.00.[203] Benefits are also minimal. This can add up to standards being compromised to get workers, and there is a great deal of turnover. Ninety-seven percent of these low-paid, low-benefit jobs are held by women.[204]

In terms of national policy, the U.S. government and families alike tend to view child care as a family problem, not a public responsibility. This is the opposite view from countries in other parts of the world that provide public child care.

Whether child care should be a public responsibility is controversial in the U.S. (at one time public schools were also controversial with the education of children viewed as a "family matter").

Conservatives believe women (not men) should stay home with their children, unless they are poor single mothers, who should definitely go to work. Liberals give lip service to child care as being in the public interest, but do little to make it a reality.

Child Care Programs in the United States: Brief History and Overview

Beginning in the 1930s, the U.S. government provided a modicum of public support for child care by offering some "back door" child care assistance through public programs meant to allow women to stay home with their children in the absence of another breadwinner.

In the Social Security system, this was (and still is) in the form of survivor's benefits. If a mother with small children became widowed, survivor's benefits assured she could stay home and care for the children herself (though initially based on the father-provider-mother-caretaker model of the 1930s, the benefit is now gender neutral).

In 1935, divorced or never-married mothers who were not widows were given entitlement to far less generous payments through the Aid to Families With Dependent Children (AFDC) program that came to be known as "welfare." It was assumed that with these payments, poor mothers would stay home and take care of their own children.[205]

Government policy changed briefly during World War II, when women were needed in the work force. The government provided child care centers, some even open at night to accommodate shift workers. But at the end of the war, the centers were abruptly closed. Female factory workers fired, and the jobs turned over to men.[206]

A modest federal tax break was enacted in 1954 for working parents with child care expenses. Programs that were viewed as educational or developmental gained support in the 1960s, when the Head Start pre-school development program (usually half-day) was implemented for children from deprived backgrounds.

In 1971 Congress passed a federal child care bill, but it was vetoed by President Nixon who called it the "Sovietization of American children." President Ford vetoed another one in 1974.

Over the years, welfare programs changed to an emphasis on getting single mothers into the workforce, with some support for outside child care that continues to the present day. Child Care Development Block Grants to the states were created in 1990 to help low-income families and those receiving or transitioning from public assistance with child care.

Virtually nothing has changed in the 21st century. We still do not have a national child care program, or even a national plan. No programs (just a few modest tax breaks) exist for non-poor families.

The programs we have for low-income parents are meager. Even though public child care funding in the U.S. goes mostly to poor families, only 14% of federally eligible children receive child care assistance.

According to the U.S. Department of Health and Human Services, the current funding level for the Child Care and Development Block Grant provides for only one out of 10 eligible children.[207] Proposed cuts in child care spending would reduce the number of children *actually receiving* child care from 2.5 million in 2003 to 2.3 million in 2009, out of over 15 million *eligible* children.[208]

The situation in the U.S. differs markedly from other countries, where child care and/or early childhood education is viewed as a public responsibility. Many countries in Europe have some form of national child care.

For example, almost 100 percent of French three-, four-, and five-year-olds are enrolled in the full-day, free *écoles maternelles*; all are part of the same national system, with the same curriculum, staffed by teachers paid good wages by one national ministry.[209]

While the U.S. is a long way from such a system, advocates argue that we should be thinking about one where most if not all children in the country can be served, even if it is not through a universal and standard model like the one in France.

Opponents of any kind of government help with child care say countries with child care have higher taxes, and taxes would surely go up in the U.S. if we followed suit.

That is probably true. But if we view what families are paying now as a "tax" that is not shared by everyone, a modest tax hike for a better system that all families could benefit from does not look so bad.

The economists Suzanne Helbrun and Barbara Bergmann have done a cost analysis for a medium level system that would provide affordable care of improved quality to families, including those in the middle class.

Using national average fees for care of children aged 0-12, they estimate the annual cost for such at plan at $46 billion per year, requiring $26.4 billion over what the federal government now spends on the low-income programs. If all 4-year-old children in the U.S. were to have access to a year-round free pre-kindergarten open 9 hours per day, that would raise the estimated cost in new money to $35.1 billion per year.[210]

The total package would cost about the same amount the Department of Defense is spending on military pay and *war contracts* (e.g. Halliburton, KBR, Blackwater) alone *every 90 days*.[211]

Questions for candidates:

What would you do to help working families with child care expenses?

What would you do to increase the availability and affordability of child care?

Do you support public funding for universal pre-kindergarten for four-year-olds? For three-year-olds?

Have you, or would you, sponsor any bills that would help working families with child care? What kind of bills specifically?

What is the next step you will take to move toward universal pre-kindergarten?

FIFTEEN

Education and Title IX

"No person in the United States shall, on the basis of sex, be excluded from participation in, be denied the benefits of, or be subjected to discrimination under any educational program or activity receiving federal financial assistance." – Title IX of the Education Amendments of 1972

With these few words added to our national body of laws, sex discrimination in educational institutions that receive federal funds became illegal. Because many private schools accept some federal money, the law covered them as well as public schools at all levels – from kindergarten through graduate school.

Title IX was needed because sex discrimination (mostly against girls and women) was rampant in many areas of education. Most people did not realize this, because in those days sex discrimination was viewed as "normal."

It was "normal" that girls could not have school sports teams; it was "normal" that girls could not be street crossing guards; it was "normal" that girls were barred from auto mechanics and boys were barred from cosmetology.

It was "normal" that medical, engineering, and law schools could refuse to admit women or limit female enrollment with strict quotas. It was also normal for girls to be expelled for becoming pregnant, and pregnant teachers to be fired when they began to "show." And a little sexual harassment was normal too – after all, "boys will be boys."

Title IX has been an overwhelming success. The numbers bear this out:

- In 1971, women were 40 percent of undergraduates overall, but could still be barred from college altogether or required to score higher on admissions tests to gain entrance.[212] By 2005 women made up 54% of undergraduate enrollments. (Gender gaps are higher than average between black and Hispanic women and men, and there are still more Asian men enrolled than Asian women.)[213]

- In 1971 women were awarded fewer than 10% of medical and law degrees and 14% of doctorates. Females are now approaching 50% in all of those areas, though they still lag significantly in engineering and computer science.[214]

- In 1971, females were 1% of dental school graduates. By 2005 they were about 40% of graduates.[215]

- In 1971, only 294,015 girls participated in high school athletics. According to the U.S. Department of Education, today over 2.7 million girls participate in high school athletics, an 847 percent increase. This has not taken away opportunities for males, who are still the majority of high school and college athletes.[216]

– The Supreme Court has ruled that sexual
harassment in the schools, either by peers or
school personnel, is illegal under Title IX.
Before, victims of harassment – including boys
– had no clear way to stop harassment or seek
justice after it happened.

Despite its obvious success, Title IX has been under
constant attack since it was passed in 1972. Though
the word "sports" does not appear in the law, Title IX
has become closely linked in the public mind with
increased opportunities for girls in athletics. Conservatives have brought lawsuits, calling it a "quota system"
and charging that it is detrimental to men, particularly
in sports programs.[*]

In 1984 during the Reagan years, the Supreme
Court issued a ruling that severely limited the scope of
the law for four years – until Congress restored it with
the Civil Rights Restoration Act of 1987.

The speaker of the House of Representatives during
President George W. Bush's first term, Dennis Hastert
(R-IL), was an ardent opponent of Title IX. An ex
wrestling coach, Hastert called Title IX a "gender-based
quota system," and said that if the Supreme Court
upheld a Title IX decision against Brown University, it
would "set a dangerous precedent." (The Supreme

---

[*]Nothing in Title IX requires schools to eliminate
men's teams. Research shows that the biggest reason
minor sports for men are dropped at the college level is
the football budget – which takes the lion's share of
athletic dollars.

Court did uphold the complaint.)

In 2005 the Bush Department of Education issued a Title IX "clarification," which allows schools to refuse to create additional sports opportunities for women based solely on email interest surveys. According to the new interpretation, failure of a female student to answer an email survey can be counted by the college as a lack of interest in participating in sports. Neither the standard nor the email survey method of limiting opportunities applies to men.

At the insistence of the Senate Appropriations Committee, the Department of Education conducted a study on the effects of the new rule in 2006, and confirmed that it had weakened the law. But the Department also refused to make any changes in the "clarification."[217]

Single Sex Education

During the first 35 years of Title IX, single-sex classes and extracurricular activities were largely limited to sex education and to physical education classes that included contact sports, because gender segregated classrooms and schools before the law was passed had been a hindrance to equal opportunity for girls.

Girls were seldom sent to flagship math and science acceleration programs or special "star" schools for high achieving students. These spots were tacitly, or sometimes openly, reserved for boys. The only single gender girl's schools tended to be those for pregnant students – with far fewer resources than even the regular classrooms afforded.

But on January 8, 2002, President Bush signed into

law the No Child Left Behind Act (NCLB), a bipartisan bill which had passed both houses of Congress with large majorities. Through a little-noticed provision, NCLB called on the Department of Education to promote single-sex schools.

In response, new Title IX guidelines were issued in 2006, effectively overturning the prohibition against gender segregated schools and classrooms. These changes were not made by Congress, but by the Bush administration's appointees at the Department of Education, underscoring once again the importance of which party is in power (see p. 11).

School districts can now set up single-sex options as long as the other sex is offered something "substantially" equal. "Substantially" is not defined, and unlike the punitive evaluation requirements for progress under NCLB generally (see below) the method for measuring success of single-sex education is undefined.

Since the requirements of Title IX were weakened, there has been a proliferation of sex-segregated schools and classrooms, though there is no consistent evidence to indicate that kids learn better in these classrooms than they would in mixed gender schools with the same resources.[218]

In other words, if mixed classrooms had the same low teacher-to-pupil ratios, increased funding, and individual student attention provided in the new segregated ones, it is likely that all the students would benefit.

Indeed there is evidence that socioeconomic status, school size, selectivity, and school resources are bigger factors than gender in the success of graduates of all-female or all-male colleges. The goal should not be to separate students by gender, but to give all students the best educational experience possible.[219]

Proponents of single-gender schools and classrooms often cite a "boy crisis," setting up an artificial school battleground between boys and girls. While boys are now behind girls in achievement, it is because girls have improved more rapidly, not because boys' achievement levels have fallen.[220]

The movement has also brought a proliferation of sex-role stereotypes back into the schools. In 2006, Livingston Parish, Louisiana, announced a plan to compel gender segregation in all classes in a formerly co-ed school. In their plan, they cited an "expert" with no education credentials who contends that "boys need to practice pursuing and killing prey, while girls need to practice taking care of babies." The plan was dropped after the American Civil Liberties Union filed suit on behalf of a girl who resisted the forced segregation.

These stereotypes can hurt boys as well. In a California experiment with dual academies, boys were seen as "bad" and taught in a more regimented way, while girls were seen as "good" and taught in more nurturing, cooperative, and open environments.[221]

Parents who now support or are considering single gender schools and classrooms should study the conservative positions on Title IX and single-sex education. Parents should also ask themselves what the term "substantially equal" means in the Bush-era regulations.

Would it be "substantially" equal to offer one gender smaller class sizes and more teachers than the other sex? What about offering the two genders different content in their classes, perhaps based on unscientific stereotypes about boys and girls?

No Child Left Behind

Besides bringing back gender-segregated classrooms, there are many other changes with NCLB – the most comprehensive education program overhaul in decades. The law increased federal funding to states by more than 24 percent in its first year. With the increased federal funding, however, came an unprecedented increase of federal mandates and sanctions.

There are now requirements placed on states to increase testing, ensure a highly qualified teacher in every classroom, and hold schools accountable for the performance of all students.

There are harsh penalties for falling short. For example, states are now allowed to replace local school personnel responsible for the failure to make what the law defines as "adequate yearly progress" (AYP).

States can also extend the school day or year, change a school's curriculum, or restructure the school and reopen it as a charter or under private management.

Since enactment of the law, there has been much national debate on its effectiveness. Most of the opposition has come from the states. A few examples:[*]

- The federal rules requiring most special education students to meet the same standards on the

---

[*]For an extensive list, see the National Education Association website `http://www.nea.org/neato day/0604/nclbtimeline.html`

same test as students with no disabilities was openly defied by the state of Texas.

– The requirements for making AYP are so strict that, of 1,262 schools which had been awarded the coveted "A" rating by the state of Florida, 827 did not meet the AYP standard.

– Utah rebuffed federal threats and ordered school officials to ignore NCLB when it conflicts with Utah's own school accountability system

– Connecticut went to federal court to preserve its student assessment system, which uses sophisticated tests every other year rather than the cheaper, blunter, yearly tests mandated by NCLB

While all parents and school districts support the NCLB goals of higher student progress, better teachers, and more school accountability, they charge that NCLB has not achieved these goals. Instead it has created schools that "teach to the test," to the detriment of real educational progress.

Many states resist federal intrusion into their school systems as well. There has been so much public outcry that 128 bills have been introduced by both Democrats and Republicans in Congress to improve NCLB. None have passed to date.[222]

There is no evidence that most provisions of NCLB have had differential effects on girls and boys, but the long-term effects of NCLB's allowing single gender schools poses a danger that schools will slip back into pre-Title IX inequities.

Candidates and parties differ on whether NCLB should be scrapped. But there is no question that the state of public education, and the educational futures of girls and boys who are channeled into segregated schools, are at stake in the 2008 elections.

Questions for candidates:

Do you support the loosening of Title IX regulations that once again allow sex-segregation in schools?

If you believe sex segregation is something that should be tried, how would you assure that girls and boys facilities, teachers, and curricula are "substantially equal.?"

Do you believe Title IX regulations weakening the requirements for athletic opportunities for girls should be overturned?

Would you vote to repeal, or significantly modify, No Child Left Behind? How?

SIXTEEN

Your Money: Taxes

Taxes are part of the dialogue in every national election, for good reason. Everyone pays taxes of some kind, whether they are rich or poor. But various taxes affect people in different ways, depending on income.

If you have a very low income, you might pay no income taxes, and in fact could get money back from the government in the form of an earned income tax credit .* You would, however, still owe payroll taxes (Medicare and Social Security).

If you are wealthy and live on investments with no salary, you do pay income taxes (and capital gains taxes if you sell any investments at a profit) but incur no payroll taxes at all.

Since most people are neither very poor or very rich, they pay a combination of taxes, including payroll, income, sales, and property taxes (non-homeowners do not escape property taxes, as the costs are passed along by landlords as part of the rent). These taxes are assessed variously by the federal government as well as states, counties, cities, and school districts.

---

*The Earned Income Tax Credit (EITC) is a federal anti-poverty tax credit designed to supplement the earnings of low income workers by reducing or eliminating their taxes. When the EITC exceeds the amount of taxes owed, it results in a tax refund to those who claim and qualify for the credit.

Individuals are not the only source of tax revenue; businesses also pay taxes. Taxes, of course, finance the various government operations, provide for government services such as police and fire protection, infrastructure such as roads and bridges, government benefits like unemployment compensation and Social Security, and wars.

Historically, the tax burden has been borne by both individuals and business in varying proportions. The corporate share is about half of what it was 40 years ago. In the 1960s, corporate taxes accounted for nearly 30% of the total taxes collected.[223] By 2006, payroll and individual income taxes accounted for 78% of total revenue, while corporate taxes had dropped to 15%.[224]

Taxes affect everyone, but they can have differential effects for women. Since women in general make less than men, taxes that are *regressive* take a bigger bite out of women's incomes.

A regressive tax is one that takes proportionately more, a higher percentage, from those with less ability to pay. Conversely, it takes proportionately less from those with greater means. The sales tax, for instance, is a regressive tax.

Here's a simple example from Dr. Ralph Estes, a business professor and scholar at the Institute for Policy Studies in Washington, D.C.

> Say your income is $15,000 a year, and you spend all of it on food, clothing, and other things subject to a 6 percent sales tax. So you pay $900 in sales tax for the year. That amounts to 6 percent of your income.
>
> Now take a wealthy family with income of $500,000 a year. They don't need all that money to

live on, so say they spend $100,000 on things subject to the sales tax. They would pay $6,000 in sales taxes. They would pay more in dollars, but remember they have a lot more dollars than you do.

Now as a percentage of income, they are paying only 1.2 percent. And that's less than a fourth of the percentage you are paying. So the person with the lower income pays 6 percent of their income in sales tax, the person with 33 times as much income pays 1.2 percent. And that percentage continues to fall as income rises.

That is exactly what we mean when we say a tax is regressive. It takes a bigger percentage bite out of the total income of those with a smaller ability to pay.[225]

Just about everyone who studies tax policy, agrees that, to be fair and equitable, taxes should overall be progressive, not regressive.[226]

A progressive tax is one that is proportionate to ability to pay. The income tax is an example of a progressive tax. Those with greater wealth or income pay proportionately more, not only a higher amount but also a higher percentage, while those with lesser means pay relatively less.

In 2008, the lowest percentage is 15% (before deductions) for incomes between $8,025 and $ 32,550, while the highest percentage is 35%, for incomes over $357,700. While income taxes are still progressive, the rate on the highest income brackets is much lower than it has been in the past.

When President Bush took office, tax cuts were high on his agenda. In his first three years in office, taxes were cut in a number of areas – the most important cuts lowered income tax rates, lowered tax rates on investment income and on capital gains, and lowered the estate tax so that it gradually reaches zero by 2010 unless Congress modifies it before then.[227]

While the Bush tax cuts do provide modest benefits to low and middle-income families, they benefit the rich disproportionately. The tax cuts are also a huge contributor to the budget deficits, which increases the national debt: A few quick facts:

- Rates were cut twice as much for households in the top 1 percent of earnings as for middle-income families. In 2004, the first year the cuts were fully phased in, those with incomes of $1.25 million got an average *tax cut* (almost $58,000) that was more than the entire average *income* ($56,200) of the middle fifth of households. Those in the middle got an average tax cut of only $1,180 per household, and their tax rate actually increased slightly from 2003.[228]

- President Bush signed the largest corporate tax overhaul in two decades in 2004. The $143 billion bill had new tax breaks for oil and gas producers, corporate farmers, and other business groups.

- The Bush cuts included a $10 billion buyout for tobacco farmers, $7.9 billion in breaks for companies with large overseas operations, and $995 million in reduced taxation on income from aircraft shipping and the leasing. News reports indicated General Electric alone could reap tax breaks measured in billions from the aircraft provisions, and even Bush's Treasury Secretary John Snow criticized it as favoring foreign operations over domestic businesses.[229]

– According to the Congressional Budget Office, the tax cuts have been the single largest contributor to the substantial budget deficits in recent years. Legislation enacted since 2001 added about $2.3 trillion to deficits between 2001 and 2006, with *half of this deterioration in the budget due to the tax cuts.* (About a third was due to increases in security spending, and only about one sixth was due to increases in domestic spending).[230]

– Based on Congressional Joint Committee on Taxation estimates, the total cost of tax cuts enacted since January 2001 is $300 billion in 2006. This means that even with the spending for the wars in Iraq and Afghanistan, the federal budget would be in surplus now if the tax cuts for the wealthy and elite had not been enacted.[231]

The reason we hear so much about "making the Bush tax cuts permanent" is that all of the individual (not the corporate) cuts are scheduled to expire in 2011. Politicians will undoubtedly characterize letting the cuts expire as a "tax hike."

But consider this: according to the Center on Budget and Policy Priorities: "Once the tax cuts are fully in effect, their annual cost will be equal to the entire annual budgets of the Departments of Education, Homeland Security, Veterans' Affairs, State, Energy, and the Environmental Protection Agency combined."

If the tax cuts are extended without offsets, balancing the budget in 2012 will require cutting Social Security benefits by 28 percent, cutting defense by 38 percent, cutting Medicare by 44 percent, or cutting every other program other than Social Security, defense, Medicare, and homeland security (including education, medical research, border security, environmental protection, veterans' programs, and programs to assist the poor) by an average of almost one-fifth.

For most Americans except the wealthiest, keeping the tax cuts at the cost of implementing any of the above options would be a bad bargain."[232]

Tax Flim-Flam

Candidates and officeholders talk a lot about taxes and the role of taxes in our society. Explaining tax policy would take a separate book, so we won't try, but here are the basics.

In general, conservatives believe in "less government," and keeping taxes low is a way to achieve that. If the government has no money, it has to shrink and cut services. This is often called "starving the beast," meaning cutting the taxes that feed social spending.[233]

Conservatives also believe everyone earning a wage or salary should be taxed at the same rate regardless of income (regressive taxation), but that income from investments should be taxed at a lower rate than income from performing a job.

Progressives and liberals generally believe taxes are necessary to achieve society's mutual goals and provide for the common welfare. They would quote Oliver Wendell Holmes, "Taxes are what we pay for civilized society." And they believe that those who are more fortunate should pay more, and progressive taxes are the fairest way to achieve this.

Red-hot tax rhetoric usually centers on "new" and "fair" tax plans. Some of these, such as flat taxes and value-added taxes, are radical departures from current tax policy. Others, such as eliminating estate taxes, are just drastic changes in current tax programs or practices. Here, briefly, is what each would likely mean for women.

> **Flat taxes:** Under this scheme, everyone pays the same income tax rate, whether they make minimum wage or CEO-level megamillions. Flat taxes are by definition regressive.
>
> Under various flat-tax proposals, the taxpayer can be an individual or business, most deductions (e.g. mortgage, child care, charitable contributions) would be eliminated, and fringe benefits would be counted as income. In some schemes, a progressive surtax could be applied to higher income levels.[234] Flat taxes, or "fair taxes," as some politicians have taken to calling them, are usually sold on the basis of simplifying tax returns and making the system more equitable.
>
> For women, already the lowest earners, it means paying the same tax rate as Morgan Stanley CEO John Mack, who earned $41.4 million in 2007, and whose company agreed to a $46 million dollar

settlement for sex discrimination. On top of that, women would most likely lose the few deductions they have, and any fringe benefits like health insurance would be taxable.

National sales tax or value-added tax: This tax is exactly what it sounds like. A federal sales tax would be instituted on top of the various state and local sales taxes. (Value added taxes amount to the same thing, though they are "hidden" because they are added at each stage of production before the consumer sees the bill.)

These taxes would replace the income tax. Again, they are highly regressive, as the rich pay much less in proportion to their income.

Sales taxes are often implemented with certain categories such as medicine and food exempted, only to be added back as people later get used to the tax and the state needs more money. These taxes also begin at low rates such as 3% – a major selling point of those pushing them – and inch up gradually.

Since all poor and most middle income people spend all their money on necessities each month, virtually 100% of their incomes are already subject to sales taxes. But they now get some relief in the form of income tax deductions and refunds, which would be eliminated under these schemes.

Eliminating "double taxation" on corporate dividends. Arguments for eliminating taxes on dividends are based on an argument that it is "double taxation." The idea is that corporations pay taxes, so when they distribute a dividend to stockholders, the money has already been taxed once and should not be taxed again.

But any taxpayer could make this same argument about sales taxes or property taxes. You've already paid income tax on the money you spend at the gas station, so paying a gasoline tax is "double taxation."

The problem with eliminating any tax is that the revenue has to be made up from other sources – meaning other taxpayers. These tax schemes overwhelmingly favor the rich. Women are overwhelmingly not the rich.

Abolishing the "death tax." "Death tax" is a term politicians use to describe the estate tax or inheritance tax. It refers to the federal tax on estates over $2 million ($4 million for a married couple) – but not the whole estate.

Taxes are due only on the portion of an estate's value that *exceeds* the exemption level. The estate tax is relevant to less than one-third of one percent of all U.S. estates.

That means that of the approximately 2.3 million deaths in 2006, an estimated 6,343 estates will pay the tax (33 people out of every 10,000).[235]

So repeal of the estate tax is of no benefit whatsoever to the great majority of Americans, because they are never going to reach the threshold for the tax in the first place.

To the contrary, doing away with the tax for the few very rich who pay it will contribute to shortfalls for the majority – shortfalls that play out in such ways as cuts in Medicaid, cuts in the women, infants, and children's feeding program, or children's health care appropriations, to name a few.

Positive Tax Changes for Women

Any plan that makes the tax system more progressive will benefit women, because women are the majority of the poor and the majority of minimum-wage and low wage workers. Even at higher levels of income, women make less than similarly situated men (see pay gap, p. 179).

But there are other ways the tax system disadvantages women, and these should be fixed. Here are a few suggestions from the Money column of Ms. magazine.[236]

> **Get marital status out of the tax code:** The "household," which is the basic tax-paying unit in the U.S. system, is specifically defined to mean married heterosexual couples or single individuals. We should redefine the tax unit so that it does not exclude gay couples or cohabiting couples.
>
> The easiest and fairest way to do this would be to follow the model used in almost all other industrialized nations, where every taxpayer is treated as an individual, regardless of the type of household. This would permanently eliminate the "marriage penalty," where married couples pay more than two similarly situated individual taxpayers.

Increase the Child Tax Credit, and apply it to all families with a payroll tax liability: Working poor women get very little help from the Child Tax Credit because it is tied to the amount they pay in income tax, which is low because their incomes are so low. Yet many still have significant payroll tax bills (Social Security, Medicare).

More than 95 percent of Americans in the bottom 20 percent of the population pay more in payroll tax than in federal income tax, so expanding the credit and applying it against payroll taxes would benefit low income women.

Institute paid family leave funded by unemployment taxes, with incentives for men to also take it: California instituted paid family leave in 2004, funded by state taxes. We should not only have a national system of paid leave, but go a step further and emulate Sweden's system. In order to get the full benefit, each parent must take a turn at caregiving – the benefit doubles if the father takes his turn.

This of course would not help single mothers, but for married couples it would go a long way toward getting men to do their fair share, leveling the playing field at home and at work.

Remove the caps on Social Security taxes, and give a Social Security credit for caregiving: The push to "reform" Social Security – the primary source of retirement income for women – by privatizing it would lessen if more money was coming into the system.

For 2008 earnings above $102,000 are not subject to payroll taxes, meaning the rich once again escape their fair share. And just as income tax policies encourage women to stay home and take care of kids, the Social Security system punishes them for it by entering a big fat zero for each year spent at home. That means a more meager retirement.

As above, to get men to take their turn, the credit could be expanded if both spouses took caregiving time off.

Revoke favorable tax treatments for institutions that discriminate against women. Courts long ago ruled that religious schools that bar blacks are not entitled to tax exemptions. Yet churches that openly discriminate against women enjoy billions of dollars in tax savings through exemptions from income and property taxes, not to mention benefitting from the largesse of contributors who get to deduct their contributions. In turn these funds are used to undermine women's rights.

Case in point: the Catholic church was one of the biggest contributors to anti-abortion referenda in the 2006 election.[237]

Tax rules also underwrite sex discrimination by allowing deductions for business expenses at places that discriminate against women. After a national controversy five years ago over the exclusion of women at

Augusta National Golf Club, where corporations spend millions entertaining clients at taxpayer's expense, Carolyn Maloney (D-NY) introduced a bill in Congress to disallow such corporate writeoffs.

The bill doesn't say "private" clubs can't keep women out, or that corporations can't entertain at such places. They just can't ask taxpayers to foot the bill.

If some of the changes we need seem far-fetched or impossible, remember this: there was a time when the income tax itself was highly controversial. The suffragists used "No Taxation Without Representation," as a rallying cry. It's time women in the 21st century did the same thing. Here are a few questions to get the discussion started.

Questions for candidates:

Do you support renewing the Bush tax cuts that overwhelmingly benefit the rich, or would you let them expire as scheduled?

Do you support a national sales tax? a VAT (value added tax)?

Do you support a "flat tax"?

Do you support a caregiver credit in Social Security?

Would you revoke corporate tax deductions for entertainment at places which discriminate on the basis or gender and race?

Would you increase the child tax credit, and would you apply it against payroll taxes as well as income taxes?

If you believe taxes should be cut generally, what programs, specifically, would you cut or eliminate to pay for tax cuts?

SEVENTEEN

Your Money: Pay Equity

The pay gap between working women and men in the U.S. continues to be one of the highest concerns of women voters. It is becoming increasingly a priority for men as well, because when one earner in a family brings in less than she should, the family suffers overall.

Though "equal pay for equal work" has been the law since 1963, disparities in pay between men and women for full-time, year-round workers are not lessening substantially, and cannot be expected to go away "naturally."

According to U.S. Census statistics released in August 2007 for full-time, year-round workers, women's earnings in 2006 were 77% of men's, leaving the wage gap statistically unchanged from the previous year.

Median earnings for women of color continue to be lower, except for Asian American women who make 93% of men's earnings. African American women make 71.8% of men's earnings, and for Latinas the percentage is 59.6%. Native American women get only 58 cents.[238]

Here are a few other quick facts:[239]

- Nationwide, working families lose $200 billion in income annually due to the wage gap between men and women. That translates to between $700,000 and $2 million for individual women over the course of their work lives.

—　If married women were paid the same as men in comparable jobs, their family incomes would rise by nearly 6 percent, and their families' poverty rates would be cut by almost 40%.

—　If single working mothers earned as much as men in comparable jobs, their family incomes would increase by nearly 17 percent and their poverty rates would be cut in half.

—　If single women earned as much as men in comparable jobs, their individual incomes would rise by 13.4 percent and their poverty rates would be reduced from 6.3 percent to 1 percent.

—　Lower earnings means lower pensions. Half of all women with income from a pension in 2002 received less than $5,600 per year, compared with $10,340 per year for men.

—　Women in "men's jobs" like the building trades that historically pay more, still get shortchanged an average of $3,446 per year.

But even these miserable numbers don't tell the whole story. The pay gap gets worse for women over their work lives, including for college graduates in high paying fields. For example, women one year out of college make 80% of men's earnings. By the time college-educated women have worked ten years, the gap has widened, with full time women workers making only 69%.[240]

The pay gap gets much worse for women who drop out of the work force, even temporarily. According to a study by the Institute for Women's Policy Research, a woman who takes off for a single year will likely never "catch up." She will earn less for up to 15 years after she returns to the workforce.[241]

There are several reasons for the pay gap, including job segregation – meaning some jobs are mostly held by men and others mostly by women. Women workers tend to be segregated into lower paying clerical and service jobs, while men dominate higher paying blue collar, management, and technical jobs.

"Women's jobs" have traditionally been seen by society as less valuable than "men's jobs," though the jobs may require the same level of skill, effort, responsibility and working conditions (e.g. shop foreman vs. clerical supervisor, or social worker vs. parole officer). But even in jobs that are dominated by women, such as teaching and nursing, *men in those fields make more.*[242]

Low minimum wages also contribute to the pay gap. Because adult women are the largest group earning the minimum wage, they are also the largest group to benefit when the minimum wage is raised. Fifty- nine percent of workers scheduled to get the increase to $7.25 by 2009 are women. Over 1.25 million single parents (mostly women) with children under 18 will benefit.[243]

While the minimum wage increase will help, it is still not enough. At $7.25 per hour, a full time worker who takes no vacation will still earn only $15,080 per year before taxes. The minimum wage is not currently indexed to inflation, so women lose ground every year it is not raised. Since September 1997, the cost of living has risen 26%, while the minimum wage has fallen in real value. After adjusting for inflation, its value is at the lowest level since 1955.[244]

There have been many studies of the gender pay gap, with conservative groups claiming that women "choose" to make less because they don't want to work as much, drop out of the workforce, or want "less risky" or "women's" jobs that pay less. But when all of these factors – and others such as education – are accounted for statistically, there is still a pay gap. Experts agree that sex discrimination is the only logical explanation.[245]

The pay gap presents many problems for women, whether they are married or single, and whether they are mothers or not. And it can become like a self-fulfilling prophecy.

If someone has to take off work to take care of a child or elderly parent in a two-earner family, it makes economic sense for the lower earner to do it, because the family will lose less income that way. And because the lower earner is almost always the woman, she usually is the one to take time off.

This means she will fall behind others at her workplace, and may be seen as a "less serious worker," damaging her opportunities for promotion.

Women without children may still be seen by management as "potential mothers" and therefore devalued at promotion time. Single mothers, of course, are at the worst disadvantage, having no partner to take up the slack when caregiving calls.

To add to the problem, the U.S. Supreme Court has made it harder for women to challenge pay discrimination.

The Bush Court overruled decades of precedent in May 2007 when it narrowed the scope of the nation's main employment law, Title VII of the 1964 Civil Rights Act.

In a truly bizarre ruling, the Court said that women who believe they are being denied equal pay must file suit within 180 days after the first instance of discrimination occurs, even if it continues for years before they find out about it.

Prior to the ruling, the law had been interpreted to mean women had 180 days to bring action from the time they *learned about* the discrimination (e.g. they had been paid less than men doing the same work for years but didn't know it). The following letter, from the plaintiff Lilly Ledbetter, says it all:

> I'm a former employee of Goodyear Tire and Rubber Company. For close to two decades, I was paid less than my male coworkers – even though I was doing the same work they were, and doing it well. The company kept the discrimination quiet and I didn't know about the pay gap until I got an anonymous note about it. Seeking to rectify this injustice, I brought Goodyear to court.
>
> A jury found that Goodyear had discriminated and awarded me more than $3 million in damages. But Goodyear appealed my case all the way to the Supreme Court and got a reversal of the jury verdict by one vote. The Court said I should have filed my complaint within six months of the original act of discrimination — even though at the time I didn't

know the discrimination was happening, let alone have enough evidence to complain.

My case set a new and dangerous precedent. According to the Court, if pay discrimination isn't challenged within six months, a company can pay a woman less than a man for the rest of the woman's career. I wonder what other forms of discrimination the Supreme Court will permit in the future.

Fortunately, the Senate is now considering the Fair Pay Restoration Act. If it passes, this bill would tell the Supreme Court it got it wrong. The bill would give all employees a better shot at a fair workplace, making it easier to ensure justice for those who have been discriminated against based on sex, race, ethnicity, religion, disability, and age.

My court case is over, but thanks to the National Women's Law Center and dedicated individuals like you, the fight against pay discrimination continues. Please join us by signing the Fair Pay Campaign Pledge. Help ensure that our daughters and granddaughters have a shot at a fair workplace and a better future.

Sincerely,
Lilly Ledbetter

The Ledbetter Fair Pay Act would essentially restore the law as it had been interpreted in the nearly 43 years prior to the *Ledbetter* ruling. While this will help women who learn they are being discriminated against in bringing legal action, it will do nothing to prevent wage discrimination in the first place.

Closing the Pay Gap

A number of solutions to the gender pay gap have been proposed. One is to prohibit discrimination in jobs requiring the same levels of skill, effort, responsibility and working conditions, even if the job titles and duties are different.

To avoid potential legal liability, employers would need to conduct internal surveys of their workplaces, evaluate them accordingly, and adjust wages for the job categories that are dominated by women (or dominated by men) that have been undervalued.

In a school district, this might translate to cafeteria servers (mostly women) being paid the same as custodians (mostly men). Even though the actual duties are quite different, the required skill level and effort are about the same.

This approach is known as *comparable worth*, and it has been used successfully in Ontario, Canada, as well as the State of Minnesota to narrow the gender wage gap. Conservatives charge that it would lead to "wage setting by the government," though there is nothing in the proposals that would require this, or even suggest it. Lowering wages for a given job category to make things equal would also be prohibited.

Another proposal is to require employers to report pay statistics by gender, race, and job category. This has been proposed by Senator Tom Harkin (D-IA) in his Fair Pay Act (a separate bill from the Ledbetter Fair Pay Act above).

The idea was also endorsed during the 2007 presidential primary campaigns by Governor Bill Richardson of New Mexico. Richardson put it this way: "Much of the inequality would be eliminated if employers reported pay data by job classification, gender, and race. That way employees would know if they were being treated fairly, and employers could see if they had a problem that needed correcting. Not anyone's salary on a bulletin board, but meaningful statistics that would let people see how they are paid as a group."[246]

With the Supreme Court already having narrowed women's options in fighting pay discrimination, the choices in the '08 elections become extremely important.

Members of Congress and the next president will need to be people who are willing to undo some of the damage, through legislation and through safeguarding women from court appointments that will further undermine their rights.

Questions for candidates:

Do you support disclosure of pay statistics by gender, race, and job category?

Do you support the Ledbetter Fair Pay Act? Are you, or would you be, a co-sponsor of the bill?

Do you support new laws to ban discrimination in pay for jobs of equal skill, effort, responsibility and working conditions, even if the jobs are different?

Do you support raising the minimum wage, and indexing it to inflation?

How would you increase women's access to non-traditional jobs?

Would you support the nomination of a judge who was known for his support of corporations or opposition to workers in employment decisions?

EIGHTEEN

Affirmative Action

The term "affirmative action" describes a number of policies that actively seek to correct the effects of discrimination in the workplace, in government contracting, and in education. In the employment context, affirmative action is the process by which the underrepresentation of certain groups, including women, in a given work force is corrected.

The rationale for affirmative action rests on the fact that white males have historically been hired and promoted in greater numbers than women and male members of minority groups, and further that women and minorities are channeled or segregated into certain job categories which often pay less and offer fewer opportunities for promotion.

Affirmative action is a part of the anti-discrimination fabric of U.S. law. Discrimination in employment on the basis of race, religion, color, national origin, or sex is illegal under Title VII of the Civil Rights Act of 1964. But while Title VII prohibits discrimination, it does nothing to change the systems that foster discrimination in the workplace and education in the first place.

Because of this shortcoming, in 1965 President Johnson signed Executive Order 11246 prohibiting discrimination, on the basis of race, color, religion, and national origin, by the federal government and private employers and universities holding federal contracts, *and* requiring them to establish affirmative action plans for hiring and equal treatment on the job. Sex was added in an amendment to the Executive Order in 1967.

Affirmative action at the federal level only applies to the government itself, and to businesses and educational institutions holding federal contracts. It does not apply to private business in general, though many companies have developed affirmative action plans because they value diversity and believe it is good for business.

Conservatives have always attacked affirmative action programs as "quotas," and have also called them "reverse discrimination" against whites, usually white males. Affirmative action does not require quotas – in fact quotas are specifically prohibited.

An affirmative action employment plan seeks to insure that a company work force is representative of the population of available qualified workers in the surrounding area; in other words, a plan that produces the same work force that would result if there were no discrimination.

In addition to general hiring goals a good affirmative action plan also includes goals for specific jobs. That's because it's possible to have a work force that technically represents the surrounding pool of workers, but is segregated by job category. An example would be a work force where the total is 50% male and 50% female, but 98% of the managers are male and 98% of the clerical workers are female.

For most jobs, affirmative action does not mean the workforce must reflect the total population of minority or female workers in a given area, since all of them are not qualified for every job. The number of women and minorities in a given position need only reflect the number of *qualified, available workers in the general pool of workers from which a company is drawing.*

For example, if women constitute 45% of the available workers in a city, an affirmative action plan for hiring unskilled workers could reasonably have a goal of 45% women in unskilled positions, since all women in the general labor market are presumably qualified for unskilled positions.

For skilled positions, only the number of qualified women in the surrounding labor market would be used as a basis for hiring goals. If it is known that 22% of the graduates of area engineering programs are women, then a reasonable affirmative action goal is 22% women for entry level hiring, and a mid-level engineering work force that is 22% female in a few years.

A plan for reaching female and minority applicants to let them know about job openings is normally included in affirmative action, since word-of-mouth advertising of openings in predominantly white male companies yields predominantly white male applicants.

Affirmative action was designed to break down the "old boy network" by encouraging personnel and procurement decision-makers to look beyond personal acquaintances, golf partners, and other insider networks. This is very important not only to job-seekers but to women- and minority-owned businesses, since there are affirmative action requirements for spreading federal contracting dollars fairly (see p. 195).

Federal affirmative action programs were reaffirmed by the Supreme Count in 1995.[247] Since then conservative attacks have shifted to the states.

Many states have affirmative action goals of their own for state employment, state contracts with private firms, and admission to state universities. (It is ironic that white females have been used as plaintiffs in some high profile lawsuits seeking to outlaw affirmative action programs in education, though white women have historically benefitted greatly from affirmative action programs not only in education, but also employment and government contracting.)

Attacks on affirmative action at the state level are in the form of ballot initiatives to outlaw the programs. The highest-profile attack is Proposition 209, passed in California in 1996.

Called the "California Civil Rights Initiative" on the ballot, Proposition 209 amended the California constitution to outlaw state affirmative action programs in public education, public employment, and state contracting. Although the constitutionality of the initiative was legally challenged, the U.S. Supreme Court denied further appeal in 1997 and let Proposition 209 stand.

Since the California initiative, two more state anti-affirmative action initiatives have been successful, in Washington State in 1998 and Michigan in 2006. The initiatives are led by one man, Ward Connerly, an African American who is very closely affiliated with contractor groups that contribute most of the money to his organization.[248]

These so-called civil rights initiatives are dishonestly named, as they are *anti-* civil rights initiatives. Most voters see the titles and mistakenly believe they will increase opportunities for minorities and women, not do away with them.

When the City of Houston changed the ballot description of a Connerly-backed city initiative to make it clear that the measure would overturn affirmative action, it was soundly defeated.

Publicity usually centers around "unfair" university admission policies, though the true target is believed to be contracting. In one sense it doesn't matter – once the initiatives pass, they apply to schools, jobs, and contracts equally. And they apply to white women as well as minority women and men, and the results are stark:

- By 2006, ten year after Proposition 209 passed, only 100 African-American students, women and men, enrolled at UCLA – 2 percent of the 4,802 total, the lowest in more than thirty years. Twenty of those 100 were recruited athletes. This occurred even though percentage of African-American applicants meeting admission requirements for the University of California system has risen steadily since 1996. Critics have labeled this "race-based exclusion."[249]

- The University of California has also noted a significant decline in the number of female faculty since Proposition 209 was implemented.[250]

- The percentage of women employed in the construction industry dropped 33 percent following the passage of Prop 209, despite an increase in the number of people employed in construction industry overall.[251]

- The effect of 209 was evident in the first year in which it affected admissions; at UC Berkeley Law School, admissions of black students dropped by 80% and Hispanic students by 50%.[252]

- In the first six years after Proposition 209, contracts to women and minority owned firms were cut in half, resulting in an estimated loss of $1.4 billion. Many have struggled to stay in business, shrinking drastically in the number of jobs they are able to provide.[253]

- In the first year after Washington state's initiative passed, the freshman class at the state university had 40 percent fewer blacks and 30 percent fewer Hispanics than the previous freshman class. And Washington has seen business drop dramatically for firms owned by minorities and women that previously qualified for set-asides.[254]

- Faculty at the University of Michigan warned, shortly before the initiative passed, that likely effects would be elimination of programs to increase female enrollment in pre-college summer recruitment programs for science, math, and vocational programs, as well as a drop in the number of females receiving scholarships in Michigan.[255]

New state ballot initiatives are planned for 2008. Women should be especially concerned about these, as their opportunities will be diminished or eliminated if the measures pass. Ward Connerly is calling his Election Day 2008 campaign, "Super Tuesday for Equal Rights." On that day, he is hoping to ban affirmative action in Nebraska, Arizona, Colorado, Missouri, and Oklahoma.[256] More states, and possibly cities, are on the horizon.

There is no question that affirmative action is still needed. The pay gap between women and men begins right after college and grows in succeeding years.[257] Job segregation remains the norm, with women concentrated in teaching, nursing, clerical and sales – relatively low paid positions when compared to "men's jobs" like technical, management, and skilled trades.

Women still comprise only 2% of the CEOs of Fortune 500 companies. Female board membership in large corporations is 14.7%, with women of color holding only 3%.[258] Minority women are also hardest hit by cuts in admissions to professional schools and also by loss of job opportunities.

Nationally, the median net worth for a white, non-Latino family is $120,900; for minority families, many headed by single mothers, it's $17,100.[259]

Women-Owned Business Set-Asides

Women in business have much at stake in the elections in 2008 and beyond, particularly those who want to contract with the federal government. The United States government spends approximately $410 billion per year contracting with private business for goods and services. It is the largest purchasing organization in the world. The bulk of these contracts go to large corporations such as KBR and Halliburton.

There have long been programs setting aside procurement dollars for small disadvantaged businesses, but women traditionally were not included unless they were members of racial or ethnic minority groups. In order not to leave women out entirely, in 1994 Congress passed a law mandating a 5% set-aside for women-owned businesses.

Six years later the goal had not been met, so in 2000 Congress ordered the Small Business Administration (SBA) to write new rules to ensure that women-owned businesses got the targeted amount. The law -- the Equity in Contracting for Women Act -- was created to improve the track record of the federal government when it came to awarding a fair share of annual procurement spending to women-owned businesses.

It took the Bush administration seven years after that to actually develop and publish the rules, finally coming out with them in December, 2007. It might not have happened at all had the United States Women's Chamber of Commerce not sued the SBA in 2004 to force the agency to follow the Congressional mandate.

When the rules did come out, female business owners were outraged. Even though the SBA's own data revealed that women got a disproportionately low number of contracts in three fourths of the 140 industries in which the agency does business, it listed only four where women-owned businesses could be preferred. One of those was furniture manufacturing – primarily done offshore.

In addition, the rules limited broad eligibility to small businesses owned or controlled by economically disadvantaged women. Contracts awarded under the program were tiny – held to $5 million or less for manufacturing and $3 million or less for other areas.[260]

A few quick facts about women-owned businesses from the National Women's Business Council.[261]

- As of 2004, there are approximately 10.6 million privately-held businesses in which women own at least 50 percent of the company. Women are majority owners in two-thirds of these companies.

- Women-owned firms continue to diversify across industries, with the fastest ownership growth rates seen in "nontraditional industries." These include construction, where female ownership increased 57% between 1997 and 2004, agricultural services (44% increase), and transportation, communications and public utilities (38% increase).

- One in five women-owned businesses is owned by a woman of color. As of 2004, 1.4 million privately-held firms were majority-owned by women of color. These firms employ nearly 1.3 million people and generate $147 billion in revenues.

- Each year women business owners lose over $5 billion dollars because of federal government failure to reach its mandated women's business contracting goals.[262]

Questions for candidates:

Do you support or oppose affirmative action in education, employment, and contracting?

How would you prevent the drastic drop in university admissions for minority students that has been shown to happen when affirmative action programs are eliminated?

What would you do to eliminate the "glass ceiling" in earnings and employment opportunities for women, particularly as they try to move up the ladder?

Do you believe in set-asides in government contracting for women-owned businesses?

Would you limit these set-asides to disadvantaged women?

How would you be sure the Small Business Administration complies with the mandate from Congress that women-owned businesses get 5% of contracting dollars?

Would you raise the amount of dollars the government sets aside for these contracts? How?

NINETEEN

Your Life: Violence

Violence in U.S. society is a problem for both women and men. While men are more often victims of physical violence, certain types of violence disproportionately affect women and children – domestic violence, stalking, sexual assault, sex trafficking, and abortion clinic bombings and harassment.

Below are a few quick facts on violence against women in the U.S.

- In a 1998 study based on a survey of 16,000 participants, equally male and female, nearly 25% of women and 7.6% of men reported having been physically assaulted and/or raped by a current or former spouse, cohabiting partner, or dating partner/acquaintance at some time in their lifetime.[263] (No follow up studies of this magnitude have been done by the government since 1998.)

- Approximately 1.3 million women and 835,000 men are physically assaulted by an intimate partner annually in the United States.[264]

- Of females killed with a firearm almost two-thirds were killed by their intimate partners, the great majority of whom were male. The number of females shot and killed by their husband or intimate partner was more than three times higher than the total number murdered by male strangers using all weapons combined in single victim/single offender incidents in 2002.[265]

– The Department of Justice reported in 2005 that 84% of spouse-abuse victims were females, and 86% of victims of dating partner abuse were female. Males were 83% of spouse murderers and 75% of dating partner murderers.[266]

– According to U.S. government statistics, Native American and Alaska Native women are more than 2.5 times more likely to be sexually assaulted than other women in the USA. In at least 86 percent of the cases, survivors report that the perpetrators are non-Native men.[267]

These few facts do not begin to describe the scope of the problem. There are many other equally shocking statistics on violence involving women and children. For details the reader is referred to the American Bar Association's Commission on Domestic Violence website at http://www.abanet.org/domviol/stat istics.html#fmi .

Stopping Violence – What We Have

The first comprehensive federal legislation responding to violence against women was introduced in 1990. The Violence Against Women Act (VAWA) took four years to pass, and was signed by President Clinton in 1994.

It established a number of discretionary grant programs for state, local, and Indian tribal governments, including grants to aid law enforcement officers and prosecutors, encourage arrest policies, stem domestic violence and child abuse, establish and operate training programs for victim advocates and counselors, and train probation and parole officers who work with released sex offenders.

VAWA also funded battered women's shelters, rape prevention and education, reduction of sexual abuse of runaway and homeless street youth, and community programs on domestic violence. In addition, it mandated several studies of violent crimes against women.

The Violence Against Women Act made a number of changes in federal criminal law. Penalties were created for stalking or domestic abuse in cases where an abuser crossed a state line to injure or harass another, or forced a victim to cross a state line and then physically harmed the victim in the course of a violent crime.

The law strengthened penalties for repeat sex offenders, required restitution to victims in federal sex offense cases, and allowed evidence of prior sex offenses to be used in some subsequent trials regarding federal sex crimes.

VAWA set new rules of evidence specifying that a victim's past sexual behavior generally was not admissible in federal civil or criminal cases regarding sexual misconduct, and that rape victims be allowed to demand that their alleged assailants be tested for HIV.

VAWA was reauthorized in 2000 and again in 2006, retaining most of the original programs and creating new ones to prevent sexual assaults on campuses, assist victims of violence with civil legal concerns, create transitional housing for victims of domestic abuse, and enhance protections for elderly and disabled victims of domestic violence.

The new version also created a pilot program for safe custody exchange for families of domestic violence, and included changes in the federal criminal law relating to interstate stalking and immigration.

Stopping Violence – What We Need

Despite the fact that almost all of the money from VAWA goes to local resources and supports the National Domestic Violence Hotline located in Texas (where Laura Bush is reported to have been a donor at one time), conservatives continue to claim it is a handout for "national feminist groups." Some want to do away with VAWA altogether.

Women's advocates must constantly defend VAWA and the national statistics on violence that are its underpinnings. Even though most of the statistics come from the federal government, conservative advocacy groups actively try to "debunk" the numbers.

Consequently, funding for VAWA is under incessant attack. In 2007 Congress clearly saw the need for increased funding and responded by passing increases for VAWA.

But President Bush's 2008 budget request proposed funding for VAWA programs at $400 million *less* than authorized by Congress in 2006. His plan also asked Congress to consolidate programs and funding into one competitive block grant open to all eligible grantees, from state governments to rural shelters.

Advocates say this ignored the Congressional intent behind each program and would create inefficiencies and competition for these already stretched funds.

Such block grants would also create a massive administrative burden on the Office of Violence Against Women and produce devastating chaos in local programs and state funding.[268]

When the appropriations bill passed in January 2008, Congress overruled the President and VAWA received a small increase of $17 million, though many individual programs were cut. For example, the Crime Victims' Fund was cut by $35 million.

Undaunted by Congress' insistence on maintaining this valuable program, the administration's 2009 budget request would cut funding for Justice Department programs designed to combat domestic violence by $100 million.

One gap in VAWA is in legal assistance to victims of domestic violence, which the law does not address. Studies estimate that fewer than one in five low-income survivors of domestic violence ever even see a lawyer. Yet legal advice is key for these women as they seek help from the police or court system.

Often, stopping the violence hinges on the ability to obtain effective protection orders, initiate separation proceedings, or design safe child custody arrangements. Without legal knowledge, these options are not accessible.

Senator Joe Biden (D-Del) has introduced The National Domestic Violence Volunteer Attorney Network Act (S.1515) that would meet this demand for legal assistance by mobilizing 100,000 volunteer attorneys willing to work on behalf of survivors of abuse. If it becomes law the act would also give the National Domestic Violence Hotline $500,000 to provide legal referrals to victims who call in requesting help.[269]

Hate crimes, those targeting victims or property as a result of bias against a particular race, religion, ethnic or national origin, are also astoundingly high. The law does not include gender, sexual orientation, gender identity, and disability. If it did, women, both gay and straight, would have an additional legal tool as victims of violent crime when gender or sexual orientation are the motivating factor.

New hate crimes laws including these categories passed both the House and Senate in 2007, but fell short of becoming law because there were not enough votes to override a threatened veto by President Bush.

With continued assaults on VAWA funding, the future of programs to combat violence against women is very much at stake in the '08 elections and beyond.

Questions for candidates:

Do you support continued full funding for the Violence Against Women Act?

Do you support The National Domestic Violence Volunteer Attorney Network Act that would provide volunteer attorneys for low income domestic violence victims?

Would you extend coverage under the Hate Crimes law to include gender, sexual orientation, gender identity, and disability?

TWENTY

Human Rights

Discrimination against lesbian women, gay men, bisexual and transgendered (LGBT) individuals continues to exist in the workplace, and in U.S. public policies and programs.

Our nation's hard-won civil rights and employment laws do not cover sexual orientation, or family formation rights for couples who are not heterosexual. This means that over 1,000 legal protections and benefits in state and federal law are inaccessible to many individuals and same- sex couples. Legal recognition of sexual orientation in employment laws would protect individuals from discrimination in the workplace.

Recognition of same-sex couples in civil codes would provide access to health care and medical decision-making for partners and their children, parenting rights, Social Security survivor benefits, equal tax treatment, and rights in inheritance, to name some of the more important benefits. It would also result in the ability to pool resources to buy or transfer property without adverse tax treatment.

Lesbians and gays cannot serve openly in the military, going back to the Clinton-era "don't ask, don't tell" policy, despite evidence that the policy is not working.[270] Nearly three in four (73%) members of the military say they are personally comfortable in the presence of gays and lesbians. Of the 20% who said they are uncomfortable around gays and lesbians, only 5% are "very" uncomfortable.[271]

As noted elsewhere in this book (see p. 53), public support for the rights of gay Americans is at an all-time high and growing. Even after the 2004 election, in which anti-gay ballot initiatives and anti-gay rhetoric reached new decibel levels, the National Election Pool's comprehensive exit poll revealed that 60% of American voters favor legal recognition of gay and lesbian couples: 25% favor marriage, and 35% favor civil unions.

Only 37% say that gay and lesbian couples should be denied any and all forms of legal recognition.[272]

The National Gay and Lesbian Task Force also reported resounding defeats for the high profile anti-gay candidates.[273] Since that time, support for gay marriage has strengthened, particularly among women, with 42% supporting vs. 32% for men.[274] Gay adoption has also gained more acceptance, with half of women and 41% of men supporting it. [275]

A very large majority of Americans believes that gays should be protected from employment discrimination. Support for equal employment opportunity has reached near-universal levels, with over 90% answering "yes" to the question: "In general, do you think homosexuals should or should not have equal rights in terms of job opportunities?"

Equal treatment in the military also receives very high support. Gallup polls have found that eight in 10 Americans now say gay men and lesbians should have equal employment rights in the U.S. military — up from 57% when the issue of openly gay servicemembers came to national prominence in 1992.[276]

Protecting LGBT people from violent crimes by including them in the definition of hate crimes (which carry additional penalties) is also widely supported. Hate crimes expansion has been proposed since 1998, the year Matthew Shepard, a gay college student, died after he was beaten and tied to a fence in Wyoming. By 68 percent to 27 percent in a Gallup Poll in May 2007, Americans favored expansion of the laws to help protect gay and lesbian people.

The Senate passed a Hate Crimes Prevention Act 65 to 33 in 2004. The House passed it by 223 to 199 in 2005. But the Republican-controlled Congress squashed the bill in negotiations.

The House passed the bill *again* in 2007 with 55% (including 25 Republicans) voting for it, but it was not enough to overcome a threatened Bush veto.[277] As of February 2008, a similar bill was once again pending in the Senate, but prospects of a veto-proof majority before the 2008 elections were slim.

Questions for candidates:

Do you support or oppose a Constitutional amendment to outlaw same-sex marriage?

Do you support or oppose legal recognition for same-sex couples with federal benefits and recognition by the states?

Do you support including sexual orientation in laws that prohibit workplace discrimination? Have you, or would you, sponsor a bill to do that?

Do you support or oppose provisions banning gay men and lesbian women from serving openly in the U.S. military?

Do you support expanding hate crimes laws to cover sexual orientation? Have you, or would you, sponsor a bill to do that?

TWENTY-ONE

Women in the Military

Almost one in seven members of the military serving on active duty are women, and they make up a nearly identical percentage of National Guard and reserve units. Since 2002, females have served nearly 170,000 tours of duty in Iraq and Afghanistan.

In these two wars, rape and sexual assault against women in the U.S. military by other soldiers as well as by contractor personnel has been identified as a serious and growing problem. Air Force general William Begert, who investigated sexual assault in the military in 2004, uncovered scores of rape accusations, a rising trend of reported abuses, and the most basic shortcomings in tracking the crime and attending to its victims.[278]

According to *The New York Times*, confidential surveys have found that up to 30 percent of women veterans reported being victimized in sexual assaults while in the military. Three out of four said they had not dared to report being assaulted because of concerns about retaliation, career advancement, and public exposure.[279]

Recently it has come out that women working for war contractors in Iraq have also been raped, with contracting companies ignoring or covering up the allegations. These women have no access to the military justice system, and the companies have required them to sign pre-employment arbitration agreements cutting off their access to the U.S. criminal justice system.

The U.S. government has been slow to investigate the allegations, and has not formulated a policy for dealing with contractor personnel who commit rape or other crimes.[280]

Despite the alarming rate of sexual assault in the military which can result in pregnancy, U.S. military women cannot obtain abortions in military facilities at home or abroad, even if they pay for the procedure with their own money.*

When deployed overseas, this could mean resorting to unsafe local facilities, or petitioning for leave to travel to a safe hospital or clinic in another country. In many foreign countries, abortion is illegal, meaning nonmilitary facilities are not available, whether safe or not.[281]

Although women have served in the U.S. military since 1901, they are the only American women whose professional advancement is artificially curtailed by government laws and policies. In the last decade, laws banning women from serving on military aircraft with combat missions and aboard combat ships were repealed, but women cannot serve aboard submarines, in infantry, armor, and most artillery units, or in special forces units.

---

*While the U.S. law banning abortions in military facilities technically has an exception for pregnancy resulting from rape, this is of no value in practice. Women cannot prove rape in time for a safe abortion, and many are afraid to bring charges in the first place.

Conservatives continue to call for outright bans on military women serving in combat, even though military leaders themselves say these bans are increasingly artificial and meaningless given today's combat realities.[282] The public supports women being able to serve in combat by a 62% majority.[283]

In addition to the problems experienced by active servicewomen, the destruction of so many military families has been one of the most tragic – and unpublicized – effects of the ongoing U.S. wars. As more military women return from fighting in Iraq and Afghanistan, they are finding that veterans' services aren't meeting their needs.

An estimated 8,000 female veterans are homeless, and others suffer from mental illness.[284] Divorces in the Army have doubled since September 11, 2001, with one in five couples separating within two years of one spouse's deployment. Women in every military branch are twice as likely to get divorced as men.[285]

Critics charge that Congress has failed to appropriate adequate money for counseling and family support services to help keep families together after the deployment has ended.

Additionally, there have been too many horror stories of women and men going away to combat, only to return and discover they have lost custody of children. This has happened because state family court judges have ruled that state family law takes precedence over the Servicemembers Civil Relief Act, the federal law that protects members of the military from such events as property foreclosures while they are away, but does not safeguard them against loss of their children.

Though the law was completely overhauled in 2003, it did not clearly spell out custody rights for service members deployed overseas. During the 2008 primary season, some candidates supported amending and clarifying the federal law to specify that it does apply in custody cases, and that a parent's absence due to a deployment cannot be used to justify permanent changes in custody or visitation.

They also advocated for ensuring that jurisdiction rests with the state where the child resided before the soldier deployed, as some non-custodial parents have moved children to more "sympathetic" states when seeking changes in custody orders.

There are serious disagreements between candidates on whether and how to end the wars in Iraq and Afghanistan. But the problems of women in the military cannot wait. Our military women deserve to be free from the threat of sexual assault, and to be treated as equals with male soldiers. Given the current reality, it is imperative that candidates give solid answers as to how they would solve problems in '08 and beyond.

Questions for candidates:

What would you do to stop the sexual harassment, rape, and sexual assault that military women are experiencing from other soldiers and contractors?

Do you think women who work for contractors who are raped should have access to the U.S. criminal justice system? The military justice system?

Do you support providing abortion services for women in the military, at military medical facilities? Have you, or would you, sponsor any bills to that effect?

Do you support allowing women to hold all military assignments for which they are qualified?

If not, are you willing to change your mind on combat restrictions for women if you see solid evidence that they are not militarily justified?

How would you help returning veterans with family problems of divorce and family violence that seem to be associated with deployments?

How would you protect military personnel from losing legal custody of their children while on deployment?

TWENTY-TWO

Global Women's Issues

In the '08 elections candidates and voters have the opportunity to spur the United States towards greater global leadership in improving the lives of women worldwide, especially in poverty stricken regions, conflict areas, and emerging democracies. Our government has in the past sometimes exercised leadership in bettering women's situation worldwide, but in recent years the efforts have stalled and in a number of areas gone steadily backward.

Reproductive Health and Family Planning

The United States began its involvement with international family planning during the Nixon administration. Since then, it has become highly politicized.

The history of the United Nations Population Fund (UNFPA) is instructive as to how family planning has become the proverbial "political football." The UNFPA was created to support family planning and reproductive health services, including maternal and child health care, in low-income countries. The United States was UNFPA's largest contributor, and we matched all other contributions in the first several years of the program's existence.

Funding cuts began in the early Reagan years, and money was cut off entirely from 1986 through the end of George H.W. Bush's term in 1992. The argument made was that the program did not comply with restrictions that had been passed by Congress in 1985, barring U.S. funding for any international organization that the *president determines* "supports or participates in the management of a program of coercive abortion or sterilization."

President Clinton restored funding to UNFPA in 1995. That year, representatives from 179 nations met at the U.N. International Conference on Population and Development in Cairo, to develop a landmark plan linking economic and social development with women's reproductive rights. They set a goal of universal access to reproductive health services by 2015 with UNFPA as the lead agency, and pledged to invest $17 billion in population programs annually by 2000.

The U.S. Congress appropriated $50 million for UNFPA but then withheld $10 million of it, stipulating that no U.S. funds could be spent in China because of its birth limitation policies.

On his first business day in office, President George W. Bush reinstated the Reagan-era "global gag rule," which prohibits the granting of U.S. funds to any overseas health clinic unless it agrees not to use its *own, private, non-U.S. funds* for any abortion-related services.

Since the main work of many of these clinics is birth control information (thereby reducing the need for abortion), women in poor countries have suffered. Lack of funds has caused many clinics to close altogether.[286]

President Bush did, however, initially support UNFPA and requested $25 million in 2001 for the program, with Secretary of State Colin Powell praising the agency for its "invaluable" work. Congress, in a bipartisan vote, appropriated $34 million for UNFPA for FY 2002. But conservative extremists mounted a campaign charging that UNFPA is complicit in forced abortions in China, and President Bush placed a hold on the UNFPA appropriation.

Despite repeated appropriations from Congress and several reports from government agencies concluding that there is no evidence that UNFPA has knowingly supported or participated in the management of a program of coercive abortion or involuntary sterilization in China, President Bush has continued to withhold funds. By 2006, the total amount allocated by Congress but denied by President Bush came to $160 million.

In addition to withholding money for UNFPA, President Bush's fiscal year 2008 budget request to Congress proposed a 25% cut to all U.S. programs promoting family planning and reproductive health overseas, despite the fact that maternal mortality remains high in many countries, and more than 200 million women want, but cannot access, modern methods of family planning.

The Women's Human Rights Treaty

The major worldwide treaty guaranteeing the rights of women worldwide is known as CEDAW, which stands for Convention on the Elimination of all Forms of Discrimination Against Women. To shortcut the unwieldy name, it is often referred to as the women's human rights treaty.

CEDAW is the most authoritative U.N. human rights instrument to protect women from discrimination. It is the first international treaty to comprehensively address fundamental rights for women in politics, health care, education, economics, employment, law, property, and marriage and family relations.

The United States is the only industrialized country in the world that has not ratified CEDAW. By not ratifying, the U.S. is in the company of countries like Iran, Sudan, and Somalia.

The CEDAW treaty was actually signed by President Carter in 1980, and sent to the U.S. Senate for ratification. To be ratified, a treaty must be reported out of the Senate Foreign Relations Committee and scheduled for a vote on the Senate floor. Once on the floor, it must pass by a two-thirds majority.

This is another case where committee control is important (see p. 15), because the committee chair can schedule hearings and committee votes to send legislation to the floor, or bottle it up without a hearing for many years.

Both Democrats and Republicans have at various times been in control of the White House and the Senate since President Carter signed the treaty. But the Senate Foreign Relations Committee has failed to act under both parties. Hearings were not held until 1990, a full ten years after Carter signed the treaty.

In 1993, sixty-eight senators signed a letter asking President Clinton to support ratification of CEDAW. After a thirteen-to-five favorable vote by the Foreign Relations Committee in 1994, a group of conservative senators then blocked a Senate floor vote.

Eight years later, in June 2002, the Senate Foreign Relations Committee held another hearing, and the Committee voted twelve to seven in favor of sending CEDAW to the full Senate for ratification. Time ran out on the congressional session before a floor vote could be scheduled, meaning the process will have to be repeated by a new Foreign Relations Committee.

Conservatives do not want the U.S. to ratify CEDAW. They say that it is a "global Equal Rights Amendment," and that it would "do away with Mother's Day." Progressives, human rights, and women's rights groups urge that it be ratified, arguing that the U.S. cannot occupy the moral high ground in global women's rights until our country signs the treaty. If the U.S. does not sign, it encourages other nations to ignore the provisions of the treaty, and thus slow or stop the progress of women worldwide.

The treaty has been used as a basis to advance women in the countries that have signed it, in areas such as providing education for girls, access to health care, political equality, the right to inherit property, and spousal rights in property ownership. All of these have helped in alleviating global poverty for women.[287]

Other Treaties

The 1995 United Nations Fourth World Conference on Women adopted what is known as the Beijing Platform for Action for Women. One provision is the recognition that women and children are particularly affected by the indiscriminate use of land mines, and the Platform urges ratification of international treaties that would prohibit these land mines.

In December 1997, the treaty banning the use, production, trade and stockpiling of antipersonnel mines was signed in Ottawa, Canada by 122 nations. Over the next ten years, 34 more countries ratified, for a total of 156 by December 2007. Signing states were mine-affected countries as well as former users and producers of the weapons, including most members of NATO. The United States is one of only 39 countries that have not yet joined. Other outliers include Russia, China, India and Pakistan.[288]

The Convention on the Rights of the Child is the most widely accepted human rights treaty. Adopted by the United Nations in November 1989, it spells out the basic human rights to which children everywhere are entitled: the right to survival; to develop to their fullest; to protection from harmful influences, abuse and exploitation; and to participate fully in family, cultural and social life.

The four core principles are non-discrimination, devotion to the best interests of the child, respect for the views of the child, and the right to life, survival and development.

The treaty protects children's rights by setting standards in health care, education, and legal, civil and social services. The Convention on the Rights of the Child has been ratified by *all* governments except two: the richest, the United States of America, and one of the poorest, Somalia.[289]

Women in Conflict Areas

Iraq and Afghanistan

"The advance of women's rights and the advance of liberty are ultimately inseparable," President George W. Bush told a group of 250 women from around the world who gathered at the White House March 12, 2004, to celebrate International Women's Day. The advance of freedom in the greater Middle East has given new rights and new hopes to women there, he noted, and the women leaders of Afghanistan and Iraq have displayed "incredible courage."[290]

To say the least, the President's view of the progress of women in both countries is warped. In November, 2007, NBC Nightly News aired a segment about a "wave of violence that's gone largely unreported lately against women in Iraq." The report noted that Iraqi women, once the most emancipated in the Arab world, are increasingly unable to work, wear cosmetics, or walk around without head to toe covering. Shiite militiamen and religious zealots are using Islam to tighten their control, murdering women for not wearing the veil or the scarf, for using makeup, or for holding a job.[291]

President Bush also promised to liberate the women in Afghanistan, and some progress was made in the initial stages of that war. But women and girls are once more being persecuted as the Taliban has gained back much of the strength it lost early in the war.

By 2006, girls' schools were routinely burned to the ground (by one estimate, one per day), and female teachers killed for "going against Islam."[292] The chief of women's affairs in Kandahar province was also assassinated in 2006, and female election workers as well as those holding voter cards have been killed.[293] And women were back in the burqua (a full body covering with mesh over the eyes) in fear of their lives. In January 2008 a journalist was sentenced to death for downloading information on women and Islam from the Internet and distributing it.

Darfur

The current plight of women in Darfur, Sudan, is one of the worst in the world. Since February 2003, when the ethnic conflict involving the Sudanese government and African and Arab tribes began, hundreds of thousands of civilians have been killed.

The U.S. government has labeled the conflict genocide against non-Arab African tribes, and the world has condemned the Sudanese government for supporting the murderous African black Arab militias known as Janjaweed. Hundreds of thousands of civilians have fled Darfur as refugees, while millions have been internally displaced. Women have been targeted for systematic and widespread murder, torture, rape, abduction, looting, and forced displacement.

On July 31, 2007, the UN Security Council unanimously authorized a hybrid United Nations-African Union force of 26,000 (UNAMID) for Darfur. According to Amnesty International, there are currently two main sets of obstacles to that deployment: deliberate obstructions erected by the government of Sudan, and lack of contributions from donor countries (including the United States) of desperately needed air and ground transport equipment, including 24 essential helicopters.

Women's advocates say the U.S. can provide money for equipment, and it can influence European and other donor countries to press the Government of Sudan to quit stalling and facilitate the deployment of UNAMID.[294]

Questions for candidates:

Do you support U.S. aid to international family planning programs? Have you, or would you, vote to fund these programs in full?

Would you support repeal of the "global gag rule" on organizations that provide legal abortion services overseas?

Would you vote to restore full funding to the United Nations Population Fund?

Do you support the ratification of CEDAW by the United States? What would you do to see that the treaty comes up for a vote?

Do you support the anti-land mine treaty, and the international treaty on the rights of the child?

Women are being persecuted in both Iraq and Afghanistan, and not allowed basic human rights by the religious police. What would you recommend the U.S. do now to help women in those countries?

What would you do to ensure the rights of women in Afghanistan and Iraq after the U.S. involvement has ended?

What would you do to end the genocide in Darfur, and specifically what would you do to protect women from rape as a weapon of the war there?

TWENTY-THREE

The Last Word – Equal Constitutional Rights

Much of this book is about threats to the rights granted to women under various laws, such as Title IX (prohibition of discrimination in educational programs) and Title VII (barring discrimination in employment), and the continuous assault on such laws by conservatives.

One reason that women must be constantly vigilant about protecting their rights under statutes and regulations is that women do not have *fundamental equal rights with men* in the U.S. – meaning equal rights under our Constitution.

Although polls show that most people believe otherwise (see p. 38), women are *not* explicitly guaranteed equal rights with men under the United States Constitution. Without having equal rights constitutionally protected, women must rely on a patchwork of laws (e.g. Equal Credit Act, Pregnancy Discrimination Act, Equal Pay Act) that can be repealed or weakened at any time by acts of Congress, or in some cases by regulations and presidential executive orders.

Additionally, courts can and have narrowed protections originally guaranteed by statute, resulting in women having to wage long campaigns with new bills in Congress to restore what's been taken away or weakened.[*]

Because equal rights are not explicitly protected in the federal Constitution, the rights women have often depend on the state in which live. For example, in every state but Montana, women still pay higher rates than similarly situated men for most kinds of insurance.

Similarly, state courts have ruled that state Equal Rights Amendments protect women's rights to reproductive services under Medicaid, but women whose states do not have ERAs are not protected.

The proposed Equal Rights Amendment is not complicated. The entire text is only 52 words:

Section 1. Equality of rights under the law shall not be denied or abridged by the United States or by any state on account of sex.

Section 2. The Congress shall have the power to enforce, by appropriate legislation, the provisions of this article.

Section 3. This amendment shall take effect two years after the date of ratification.

---

[*]Title IX is a case in point. The *Grove City v. Bell* decision in 1984 declared that only individual programs receiving federal funds were subject to the law banning discrimination in educational programs, not institutions as a whole. Women's groups had to mount a four-year fight to pass legislation overturning *Grove City* and restoring the original intent.

The Equal Rights Amendment embodies a simple concept that had the blessing of both political parties until the Republicans struck it from their platform in 1980. The Democrats followed suit in 2004.

For an amendment to become part of the Constitution, it must be passed by a 2/3 majority in each chamber of Congress and then sent to the states for ratification. Each state votes on ratification separately, and an amendment cannot become part of the Constitution unless it is ratified by three-fourths of the states.

The Equal Rights Amendment was first introduced in Congress in 1923, on the heels of the ratification of the 19th Amendment giving women the right to vote. It was finally passed out of Congress and sent to the states in 1972, with a seven year deadline for ratification (later extended three years). The deadline was not in the amendment, but the preamble, causing some scholars to make the argument that it is non-binding.

The ratification drive succeeded in 35 states, but 38 were needed for it to become part of the Constitution. The ERA has been reintroduced in every Congress since, but has never been put to a vote.

The Equal Rights Amendment has recently been renamed the Women's Equality Amendment and introduced as such by its chief sponsors, Carolyn Maloney (D-NY) and Edward Kennedy (D-MA). Though it has a high number of co-sponsors (25% of the Senate and almost 50% of the House members have signed on), it has not been scheduled for committee hearings which could lead to floor votes in Congress.

Conservatives argue that equal constitutional rights will result in "abortion on demand" and "unisex toilets," though the amendment mentions neither. When they're not raising the specter of unisex toilets (guess they've never been on an airplane), conservatives also argue that a new amendment isn't needed because the "equal protection under the law" clause of the Fourteenth Amendment already guarantees equal rights for women.

This is not true. The Fourteenth Amendment was passed to protect African American men from discrimination. Courts have failed to take sex discrimination as seriously (what lawyers call *level of scrutiny*) as race discrimination under the Fourteenth Amendment, even when the letter of the law is explicit.[295]

The result has been that many discriminatory practices – barring women from certain military jobs, establishing boys-only public classrooms and schools, and openly discriminating against women in insurance programs to name a few – are still legal.

Women in the U.S. lag far behind women in the rest of the world when it comes to constitutional equality. Most individual countries in Europe have formalized equal rights for women in their constitutions, and equal rights are included in the pending European constitution. Women have had equal constitutional rights in Japan since 1946, and the constitutions of many other countries worldwide declare women as legal equals to men.

Since the 1990s, new constitutions in countries like Mozambique, Namibia, Ethiopia, Malawi, Uganda, South Africa, Rwanda, Burundi, and Swaziland have included non-discrimination or equality provisions, prohibiting customary practices if they undermine undermined the dignity, welfare or status of women.

With neither party having equal rights for women in their platform, it is especially important to confront candidates in every election as to their intentions regarding the Women's Equality Amendment.

Questions for candidates:

Do you support the Women's Equality Amendment to the U.S. Constitution?

Have you, or would you, co-sponsor the amendment in Congress?

Would you push for hearings and a congressional vote on equal rights for women?

Do you think equal rights for women should be a part of your party's platform?

Until equal rights for women are in the Constitution, will you pledge to work to eliminate unequal treatment of women in all forms, all domains, and all legislation?

The Political Parties and Their Platforms

Party platforms are revisited in presidential election years, and voted on at the national party conventions. While there are some changes every four years, general philosophy is highly consistent and the wording is often nearly identical to the previous platform.

Since the 2008 platforms will not be adopted by the parties until after publication of this book, we present excepts from the 2004 platforms. These can serve as a reliable guide to how the '08 platforms will look. All quotes below are verbatim, and are presented without comment. Issues (our captions)[*] are in alphabetical order, with platform page numbers noted in parentheses.

2004 Republican Party Platform:
A Safer World and a More Hopeful America

Abortion:

The unborn child has a fundamental individual right to life which cannot be infringed. We support a human life amendment to the Constitution and we endorse

---

[*]Categories and csptions between platforms are not a perfect match since platforms differ slightly on issues they address.

legislation to make it clear that the 14th Amendment's protections apply to unborn children. We oppose using public revenues for abortion and will not fund organizations which advocate it. We support the appointment of judges who respect traditional family values and the sanctity of innocent human life. (86) We support doubling abstinence education funding. We oppose school-based clinics that provide referrals, counseling, and related services for contraception and abortion. (82-83)

Abstinence-Only Education:

Therefore, we support doubling abstinence education funding. We oppose school-based clinics that provide referrals, counseling, and related services for contraception and abortion. (81)

Affirmative Action:

We believe in the principle of affirmative access-taking steps to ensure that disadvantaged individuals of all colors and ethnic backgrounds have the opportunity to compete economically. We support a reasonable approach to Title IX that seeks to expand opportunities for women without adversely affecting men's athletics. Because we are opposed to discrimination, we reject preferences, quotas, and set-asides based on skin color, ethnicity, or gender. (76-77)

Civil Liberties/Domestic Surveillance:

The Patriot Act is being used to track terrorist activity and to break up terror cells. Now, the FBI can use tools that have been long available to fight organized crime and drug trafficking, but could not be used in the past to fight terrorism. Intelligence and law enforcement officials are sharing information as never before. (4) [Homeland Security] The PATRIOT Act gives law enforcement and intelligence agents the tools that have long been available to fight organized crime and drug trafficking. It also made it possible for law enforcement and intelligence agents to share information and coordinate efforts to prevent terrorism. (13)

Families and Children:

We believe that every child deserves the chance to be born and grow up in a loving family. We also believe that while families exist in many different forms, there are ideals to strive for. Evidence shows us that children have the best chance at success when raised by a mother and a father who love and respect each other as well as their children. (81)

Federal Funds to Religious Groups:

No organization should be disqualified from receiving federal funds simply because it displays religious symbols, has a statement of faith in its mission statement, or has a religious leader on its board. The federal government is ending discrimination against faith-based organizations and now welcomes these groups as partners and allies in the effort to deliver social services to people in need. As a result of the President's leadership, the federal government is ending discrimination against faith-based organizations and now welcomes these groups as partners and allies in the effort to deliver social services to people in need. (75-76)

Gay Marriage/Domestic Partnership:

After more than two centuries of American jurisprudence, and millennia of human experience, a few judges and local authorities are presuming to change the most fundamental institution of civilization, the union of a man and a woman in marriage. Attempts to redefine marriage in a single state or city could have serious consequences throughout the country, and anything less than a Constitutional amendment, passed by the Congress and ratified by the states, is vulnerable to being overturned by activist judges. We strongly support a Constitutional amendment that fully protects marriage, and we [oppose] forcing states to recognize other living arrangements as equivalent to marriage. We believe that legal recognition and the accompanying benefits afforded couples should be preserved for that unique and special union of one man and one woman which has historically been called marriage. (83)

In some states, activist judges are redefining the institution of marriage. We believe that the self-proclaimed supremacy of these judicial activists is antithetical to the democratic ideals on which our nation was founded. (78-79)

We strongly support President Bush's call for a Constitutional amendment that fully protects marriage, and we believe that neither federal nor state judges nor bureaucrats should force states to recognize other living arrangements as equivalent to marriage. (83)

Gays and Lesbians in the Military

We affirm traditional military culture, and we affirm that homosexuality is incompatible with military service. (18)

Gun Control:

We applaud those seeking to stop frivolous lawsuits against firearms manufacturers which is a transparent attempt to deprive citizens of their 2nd Amendment rights. We oppose federal licensing of law abiding gun owners & national gun registration as a violation of the 2nd Amendment and an invasion of privacy of honest citizens. (74)

Health Care:

We reject any notion of government-run universal health care. We applaud efforts by President Bush and the Republican Congress to reform the broken medical liability system that is raising health care costs. (64)

Republicans are dedicated to pursuing women's health care initiatives that include access to state-of-the-art medical advances and technology; equality for women in the delivery of health care services; medical research that focuses specifically on women; appropriate representation of women in clinical trials; expanded access to prevention, screening, health promotion, chronic care, and disease management services; and direct access to women's health providers. (65)

Iraq:

Saddam had capability to reconstitute his weapons programs. While the stockpiles of weapons of mass destruction we expected to find in Iraq have not yet materialized, we have confirmed that Saddam Hussein had the capability to reconstitute his weapons programs and the desire to do so. Our nation did the right thing, and the American people are now safer because we and our allies ended the brutal dictatorship of Saddam Hussein. (8)

Long-term Care:

We support proposals by President Bush and Republicans in Congress to recognize and reward individual responsibility and compassion by creating an above-the-line tax deduction for premiums of long-term care insurance and allowing an additional personal tax exemption for taking care of an elderly parent at home. (67)

Marriage Promotion and Welfare Reform:

We endorse President Bush's plan to extend the benefits of welfare reform by strengthening work requirements and promoting healthy marriages, and offering training, transportation, and child care services to help people become self-sufficient. (82)

Pre-emptive War Power:

We therefore believe that to forestall or prevent hostile acts by our adversaries, the United States must, if necessary, act preemptively. (12)

Social Security:

Personal retirement accounts must be the cornerstone of strengthening and enhancing Social Security. Each of today's workers should be free to direct a portion of their payroll taxes to personal investments for their retirement. (40)

Stem Cell Research:

We strongly support the President's policy that prevents taxpayer dollars from being used to encourage the future destruction of human embryos. (68)

Taxes:

We believe that good government is based on a system of limited taxes and spending. Furthermore, we believe that the federal government should be limited and restricted to the functions mandated by the United States Constitution. The taxation system should not be used to redistribute wealth or fund ever-increasing entitlements and social programs. (39) Because of the vital role of religious and fraternal benevolent societies in fostering charity and patriotism, they should not be subject to taxation. (46)

Women in Afghanistan:

Today, Afghanistan is a world away from the nightmare of the Taliban. Boys and girls are being educated. Women are respected. A threat has been removed, and the American people are safer. (6-7)

Women in Combat

We support the advancement of women in the military, support their exemption from ground combat units, and support the implementation of the recommendations . . . that co-ed basic training be ended. (18)

The 2004 Democratic Party Platform: Stronger at Home, Respected in the World

Abortion:

Because we believe in the privacy and equality of women, we stand proudly for a woman's right to choose, consistent with *Roe v. Wade*, and regardless of her ability to pay. We stand firmly against Republican efforts to undermine that right. At the same time, we strongly support family planning and adoption incentives. Abortion should be safe, legal, and rare. (36)

Affirmative Action:

We support affirmative action to redress discrimination and to achieve the diversity from which all Americans benefit. (35)

Civil Liberties/Domestic Surveillance/Civil Rights:

And so we must be on constant guard not to sacrifice the freedom we are fighting to protect. We will strengthen some provisions of the Patriot Act, like the restrictions on money laundering. And we will change the portions of the Patriot Act that threaten individual rights, such as the library provisions, while still allowing government to take all needed steps to fight terror. Our government should never round up innocent people only because of their religion or ethnicity, and we should never stifle free expression. We believe in an America where freedom is what we fight for - not what we give up. (18)

We will restore vigorous federal enforcement of our civil rights laws for all our people, from fair housing to equal employment opportunity, from Title IX to the Americans with Disabilities Act. (35)

We will enact the bipartisan legislation barring workplace discrimination based on sexual orientation. (35)

Equal Pay:

We believe a day's work is worth a day's pay, and at a time when women still earn 77 cents for every dollar earned by men, we need stronger equal pay laws and stronger enforcement of them. (35)

Families and Children:

Family is the center of everyday American life. Our parents are our first protectors, first teachers, first role models, and first friends. Parents know that America's great reward is the quiet but incomparable satisfaction that comes from building their families a better life. Strong families, blessed with opportunity, guided by faith, and filled with dreams are the heart of a strong America. (27)

Gay Marriage:

We support full inclusion of gay and lesbian families in the life of our nation and seek equal responsibilities, benefits, and protections for these families. In our country, marriage has been defined at the state level for 200 years, and we believe it should continue to be defined there. We repudiate President Bush's divisive effort to politicize the Constitution by pursuing a "Federal Marriage Amendment." Our goal is to bring Americans together, not drive them apart. (36)

Gays and Lesbians in the Military:

We are committed to equal treatment of all service members and believe all patriotic Americans should be allowed to serve our country without discrimination, persecution, or violence. (35)

Gun Control:

We will protect Americans' Second Amendment right to own firearms, and we will keep guns out of the hands of criminals and terrorists by fighting gun crime, reauthorizing the assault weapons ban, and closing the gun show loophole, as President Bush proposed and failed to do.(18)

Health Care:

We will help businesses cope with the skyrocketing cost of health care by reforming our health care system & cutting taxes to help small businesses pay for health insurance. Retiree health costs impose major burdens on many employers, particularly manufacturers, and we will push for reform so that companies are not forced to choose among retirees, current workers, and their own ability to compete. (21)

We will provide tax credits to Americans who are approaching retirement age and those who are between jobs so they can afford quality, reliable coverage. We will expand coverage for low income adults through existing federal-state health care programs. And we will provide all Americans with access to the same coverage that members of Congress give themselves. (28)

We will also work to ensure that women have access to the best medicines and state-of-the-art prevention and detection techniques to stop diseases early. We will also support prevention of illness through better nutrition and exercise. (33)

Iraq:

[The Bush] Administration badly exaggerated its case, particularly with respect to weapons of mass destruction and the connection between Saddam's government and al Qaeda. This Administration did not build a true international coalition. This Administration disdained the United Nations weapons inspection process and rushed to war without exhausting diplomatic alternatives. Ignoring the advice of military leaders, this Administration did not send sufficient forces into Iraq to accomplish the mission. And this Administration went into Iraq without a plan to win the peace. (8)

Social Security:

We oppose privatizing Social Security or raising the retirement age. We oppose reducing the benefits earned by workers just because they have also earned a benefit from certain public retirement plans. (23-24)

Stem Cell Research:

Stem cell therapy offers hope to more than 100 million Americans who have serious illnesses-from Alzheimer's to heart disease to juvenile diabetes to Parkinson's. We will pursue this research under the strictest ethical guidelines, but we will not walk away from the chance to save lives and reduce human suffering. (29)

Taxes:

Today's tax law provides big breaks for companies that send American jobs overseas. Current "deferral" policies allow American companies to avoid paying American taxes on the income earned by their foreign subsidiaries. [Our candidates] will end deferral that encourages companies to ship jobs overseas, and they will close other loopholes to make the tax code work for the American worker. They'll use the savings to offer tax cuts for companies that produce goods and create jobs here at home. (20)

With the middle class under assault like never before, we simply cannot afford the massive Bush tax cuts for the very wealthiest. (23) We will roll back the Bush tax cuts for those making more than $200,000. (25)

Many American corporations today pay less than ever in taxes because of tax loopholes secured by powerful lobbyists. We will end corporate welfare as we know it. We will eliminate the indefensible loopholes in our tax code- from tax deals that have no purpose but avoiding taxes to the very shelters that Enron used to drive so many lives toward financial ruin. And we will eliminate the corporate subsidies that waste taxpayer dollars and undermine fair competition. (25)

Welfare:

We must match parents' responsibility to work with the real opportunity to do so, by making sure parents can get the health care, child care, and transportation they need. And we must expect increased responsibility from fathers as well as mothers by increasing child support enforcement and promoting responsible fatherhood together with religious and civic organizations. (22)

Notes

1. Sherr, Lynn. *Failure is Impossible: Susan B. Anthony in Her Own Words*. New York: Times Books, Random House, 1995.

2. Flexner, Eleanor. *Century of Struggle: The Woman's Rights Movement in the United States*. Cambridge, Massachusetts: The Belknap Press of Harvard University Press, 1959, 1975.

3. Center for American Women and Politics. *Gender Differences in Voter Turnout, Fact Sheet*. (2005). Retrieved January 15, 2008 from `http://www.cawp.rutgers.edu/Facts/genderdiff.pdf`

4. "Women Voters Made the Difference in 2006 Election," *Ms. Magazine* press release, November 17, 2006.

5. National Journal. *Women in the House*. Retrieved Dec. 31, 2007 from `http://nationaljournal.com`

6. U.S. Senate, roll call votes, 108th Congress, 1st session, Retrieved December 15, 2007 from `http://www.senate.gov`

7. Sullivan, Patricia. "Anne Gorsuch Burford, 62, Dies; Reagan EPA Director." *Washington Post*, July 22, 2004: B06.

8. Sydell, Laura. "Clarence the Credible, How Journalists Blew the Thomas Story." *Fairness and Accuracy in Reporting, Extra!*, 1992: Special Issue on Women.

9. U.S. Department of Human Services. *Donna E. Shalala, Ph.D., Secretary of Health and Human Services.* Retrieved November 15, 2007 from `http://www.surgeongeneral.gov/library/yout hviolence/shalala.htm`

10. Barnes, Robert. "Over Ginsburg's Dissent, Court Limits Bias Suits." *Washington Post*, May 30, 2007: A01.

11. Lee, Christopher. "Birth-Control Foe To Run Office on Family Planning." *Washington Post*, October 17, 2007: A15 .

12. Berkowitz, Bill. " Wade Horn Cashes Out." *Media Transparency*, April 25, 2007. Retrieved December 1, 2007 from `http://www.mediatransparency.org/story.php ?storyID=190`

13. Barnes, Robert. "Roberts Court Moves Right, But With a Measured Step." *Washington Post*, April 20, 2007: Page A03.

14. Risen, James. "White House Is Subpoenaed on Wiretapping." *New York Times*, June 28, 2007.

15. Roberts, John. *Tobacco executive goes public over company lies.* (February 3, 1996). Retrieved December 1, 2007 from `http://www.bmj.com/cgi/content/full/312/70 26/267/a`

16. Broder, John M. "Industry Flexes Muscle, and Weakened Bill Passes Senate." *New York Times*,

December 14, 2007: A23.

17. Tripp, Aili Marie. "Debating Women's Rights and Customary Law in Africa Today." Conference paper, Indiana University School of Law, March 2007.

18. Interparliamentary Union. *Women in National Parliaments.* (September 2006). Retrieved December 1, 2007, from
`http://www.ipu.org/wmn-e/arc/classif300906.htm`

19. Christensen, Martin K.I. *Worldwide Guide to Women in Leadership 2007.* Retrieved January 2, 2008 from
`http://www.guide2womenleaders.com`

20. Polochek, Soloman and Jun Xiang. *The Gender Pay Gap: A Cross-Country Analysis.* State University of New York at Binghamton, 2006. Retrieved January 2, 2008 from
`http://client.norc.org/jole/SOLEweb/Polachek.pdf`

21. U.S. Census Bureau, 2007, as referenced by John Edwards '08 website. Retrieved November 25, 2007 from
`http://www.johnedwards.com/women/`

22. Bureau of Labor Statistics, 2007, as referenced by John Edwards '08 website. Retrieved November 25, 2007 from `http://www.johnedwards.com/women/`

23. Heymann Jody, Alison Earle, Jeffrey Hayes. *How Does the United States Measure Up?* Institute for Health and Social Policy, McGill University, 2007.

24. "U.S. stands apart from other nations on maternity leave," The Associated Press, July 26, 2005.

25. Heymann et. al.

26. Catalyst. 2007 *Catalyst Census of Women Board Directors of the Fortune 500.* Retrieved January 2, 2008 from
http://www.catalystwomen.org/knowledge/200
7wbd.shtml

27. "NAWBO Urges SBA to Ensure WBOs Receive Fair Share of Contracts," National Association of Women Business Owners, May, 2007.

28. "Dollars, Not Sense: Government Contracting Under the Bush Administration," United States House of Representatives Committee on Oversight and Government Reform, June 19, 2006.

29. Dey, Judy Goldberg, and Catherine Hill. *Behind the Pay Gap*, Washington, D.C. American Association of University Women Educational Foundation, 2007.

30. National Science Foundation. *Women, Minorities, and Persons with Disabilities in Science and Engineering 1995-2005.* Retrieved January 4, 2008 from
http://www.nsf.gov/statistics/wmpd/pdf/tab
b-9.pdf

31. Dean, Cornelia. "Computer Science Takes Steps to Bring Women to the Fold." *New York Times*, April 17, 2007.

32. Jones, Leigh."Fewer Women Are Seeking Law." *The National Law Journal*, October 2, 2007.

33. Leonhardt, David. "Gender Pay Gap, Once Narrowing, Is Stuck in Place." *New York Times*, December 24, 2006.

34. National Association of Child Care Resource &
Referral Agencies. *Child Care in America.* (2007).
Retrieved January 3, 2008 from
`http://www.naccrra.org/news/program.php?Pa`
`ge=6`

35. Retrieved January 5, 2008 from
`http://zfacts.com/p/716.html#3033`

36. "U.S. Child Care Seriously Lags Behind that of Europe." *American Sociological Association News*, November
18, 2002.

37. Mezey, Parrott, Greenberg, and Fremstad. *Reversing
Direction on Welfare Reform: President's Budget Cuts Child
Care for 300,000 Children.* Washington, D.C.: Center on
Budget and Policy Priorities, Center for Law and Social
Policy, 2004.

38. National Women's Law Center. *National Report:
Women's Access to Health Care Services.* (2007). Retrieved
January 5, 2008 from
`http://hrc.nwlc.org/Reports/National-Repor`
`t-Card.aspx`

39. Ibid.

40. Center for Disease Control and Prevention.
HIV/AIDS among Women. (June, 2007). Retrieved
January 3, 2008 from
`http://www.cdc.gov/hiv/topics/women/resour`
`ces/factsheets/women.htm`

41. "World: HIV/AIDS Having Increasing Impact On
Women." Radio Free Europe, December 1, 2004.

42. *Women and Long Term Care.* Washington, D.C.:
Older Women's League, 2007.

43. Ibid.

44. Ibid.

45. Tolchin, Martin. "Other Countries Do Much More for Disabled." *New York Times*, March 29, 1990.

46. "Your Retirement Benefit: How It Is Figured," SSA Publication No. 05-10070, January 2008. U.S. Social Security Administration, Social Security Online, Retrieved February 16, 2008 from
http://ssa-custhelp.ssa.gov/

47. "Social Security Programs Throughout the World: Europe, 2006." Washington, D.C.: U.S. Social Security Administration Office of Policy, 2007.

48. Ibid.

49. "Social Security Programs Throughout the World: Asia and the Pacific, 2006." Washington, D.C.: U.S. Social Security Administration, Office of Policy, 2007.

50. *National Report: Women's Access to Health Care Services.*

51. *Seventh United Nations Survey of Crime Trends and Operations of Criminal Justice Systems, covering the period 1998 - 2000.* United Nations Office on Drugs and Crime, Centre for International Crime Prevention, as cited on NationMaster.com. Retrieved January 4, 2008.

52. Human Rights Watch. *CEDAW: The Women's Rights Treaty.* (2007). Retrieved January 4, 2008 from
http://www.hrw.org/campaigns/cedaw/#CEDAW%20HISTORY

53. Amnesty International USA. *Children's Rights: Convention on the Rights of the Child.* (2007). Retrieved January 4, 2008 from `http://www.amnestyusa.org/`

54. *The Mine Ban Treaty and the US Government: 10 Years and Waiting, United States Campaign to Ban Landmines.* Retrieved December 31, 2007 from `http://www.banminesusa.org/`

55. All results in this section from "Women's Movement Worthwhile." CBS News Poll, October 2005.

56. "Women in the 2006 Elections." Washington, D.C.: Lake Research Partners, November 13,2006.

57. "Women's Movement Worthwhile."

58. Opinion Research Corporation, national poll commissioned by the ERA Campaign Network, July 6–9, 2001.

59. *The Independents.* Retrieved February 15, 2008 from `http://www.WashingtonPost.com`

60. "An Even More Partisan Agenda for 2008, Election-Year Economic Ratings Lowest Since '92." Pew Research Center for People and the Press, January 24, 2008.

61. "Trends in Political Values and Core Attitudes: 1987-2007." The Pew Research Center for People and the Press, March 22, 2007.

62. Eleanor Smeal. "Women Voted for Change." *Ms Magazine*, Winter 2007.

63. "Women in the 2006 Elections."

64. "Trends in Political Values and Core Attitudes: 1987-2007."

65. "ABC News Poll." ABCNEWS.com, January 22, 2008.

66. "Abortion a More Powerful Issue for Women." The Pew Research Center for People and the Press, April 2004.

67. Ibid.

68. "Less Opposition to Gay Marriage, Adoption and Military Service." The Pew Research Center for the People and the Press, March 22, 2006.

69. "Tolerance for Gay Rights at High-Water Mark." Gallup News Service, May 29, 2007.

70. Unpublished data provided by The Pew Research Center for People and the Press, February, 2008.

71. "Less Opposition to Gay Marriage, Adoption and Military Service."

72. "Trends in Political Values and Core Attitudes: 1987-2007."

73. "Little Boost for Gun Control or Agreement on Causes Va. Tech Shootings." The Pew Research Center for People and the Press, April 23, 2007.

74. "Women in the 2006 Elections."

75. "Women's Movement Worthwhile."

76. "Women in the 2006 Elections." Washington, D.C.: Lake Research Partners, November 17, 2006.

77. "Less Opposition to Gay Marriage, Adoption and Military Service." The Pew Research Center for People and the Press, Released: March 22, 2006.

78. "Focus: Public Opinion & Polls." Gay & Lesbian Alliance Against Defamation, 2008.

79. ABC news. *Most Oppose Gay Marriage; Fewer Back an Amendment.* (May 31-June 4, 2006). Retrieved January 8, 2008 from
`http://abcnews.go.com/US/Politics/Story?id=2041689&page=3`

80. "Less Opposition to Gay Marriage, Adoption and Military Service."

81. *CBS News/New York Times Poll.*

82. Hart, Peter and Bill McInturff Polling Organizations. *NBC News/Wall Street Journal Poll.* (Nov. 1-5, 2007). Retrieved December 30, 2007 from
`http://www.Pollingreport.com`

83. Paral, Rob. *Playing Politics on Immigration: Congress Favors Image over Substance in Passing H.R. 4437.* (February 27, 2006). Retrieved December 30, 2007 from
`http://www.ailf.org/ipc/policybrief/policy brief_2006_playingpolitics.shtml`

84. National Immigration Forum. *Immigration Reform Polling Summary: Public Support for Comprehensive Immigration Reform.* (April 3, 2006). Retrieved December 30, 2007 from

http://immigrationforum.org/DesktopDefault
.aspx?tabid=148

85. *CBS News/New York Times Poll.*

86. Hill, David."Lesson: immigration is a dud issue." *The Hill Newspaper*, February 12, 2008.

87. United for a Fair Economy, as quoted in *Federal Estate Tax Background, Estate Tax Repeal Looks Unlikely as of August 2007.* Retrieved December 29, 2207 from http://www.results.org/website/article.asp?id=2022

88. Feminist Majority Foundation. *How the Gender Gap Shaped Election 2000, Preliminary Report.* (January 24, 2001). Retrieved January 2, 2008 from https://feminist.org/research/ggap2000.pdf

89. *Guns: compilation of national polls on gun control.* Retrieved Dec. 31, 2007 from PollingReport.com

90. *ABC News/Washington Post Poll. Sept. 4-7, 2007.* Retrieved Dec. 31, 2007 from PollingReport.com

91. *The Harris Poll.* (July 6-9, 2007). Retrieved Dec. 23, 2007 from PollingReport.com

92. Johnson, David C. *The Attack on Trial Lawyers and Tort Law.* Menlo Park: The Commonweal Institute, October, 2003.

93. Peter D. Hart Associates. *Civil Justice Issues and the 2008 elections.* (July 11, 2007). Retrieved Dec. 23, 2007 from http://www.atla.org/pressroom/CJSPollMemo.pdf

94. *Problems and Priorities, compilation of national polls on possible election issues.* Retrieved Dec. 18, 2007 from `PollingReport.com`

95. "Taliban Attacks on Afghan Girls' Schools Increase." *Feminist Daily News Wire*, July 12, 2006.

96. Whitaker, Brian." Taliban murders voters to derail election." London, *The Guardian*, June 28, 2004.

97. *Operation Enduring Freedom, Coalition Casualties by Year.* Retrieved February 8, 2008 from `http://www.icasualties.org/oef/`

98. Hanley, Charles J. "Piecing together the story of the weapons that weren't." The Associated Press, Posted September 2, 2005. Updated September 6, 2005.

99. *Iraqi women: Prostituting ourselves to feed our children.* (August 16, 2007). Retrieved December 31, 2007 from `http://www.cnn.com/2007/WORLD/meast/08/15/iraq.prostitution/index.html`

100. *Poll: Americans less positive on Iraq.* (July 1, 2003). Retrieved December 31, 2007 from `CNN.com`

101. "Poll: 70% believe Saddam, 9-11 link." Associated Press, September 6, 2003.

102. "Iraq Prison Scandal Hits Home, But Most Reject Troop Pullout 76% Have Seen Prison Pictures; Bush Approval Slips." Pew Research Center for People and the Press, May 12, 2004.

103. "Women in the 2006 Elections." Washington, D.C.: Lake Research Partners, November 17, 2006.

104. *Iraq Coalition Casualty Count*. Retrieved Feb. 8, 2008 from
http://www.icasualties.org/oif/default.asp x

105. CNN/Opinion Research Corporation Poll. Dec. 6-9, 2007.

106. "Meet the Press," ABC News, January 6, 2008.

107. *Statement on the Treasury Surplus - Brief Article*. Weekly Compilation of Presidential Documents. (September 21, 2000). Retrieved January 2, 2008 from findarticles.com

108. United States Treasury Department, October 11, 2007.

109. "Kennedy on Bush Veto of Labor HHS Bill." Press Release, Senator Edward Kennedy, November 13, 2007.

110. Burk, Martha. "Gender Budgets, Anyone?" *Ms. Magazine*, Winter, 2008.

111. Leland, John. "Baltimore Finds Subprime Crisis Snags Women." *New York Times*, January 15, 2006.

112. Ibid.

113. *US Mortgage Defaults Leveling Off but Repos Rising*. Retrieved February 17, 2008 from http://www.researchrecap.com/index.php/200 7/11/29/us-mortgage-defaults-leveling-off-but-repos-rising/

114. Cornett, Brandon. "Subprime Mortgage Crisis Explained," Home Buying Institute, December 18, 2007.

115. Aversa, Jeannine. "Majority Believe US in Recession." Associated Press, Feb. 10, 2008.

116. "As Talk of Recession Grows, Republicans and Democrats Differ on Response," *New York Times*, January 15, 2008.

117. Weisman, Jonathan. "Congress Approves Stimulus Package." *Washington Post*, February 8, 2008: Page A01.

118. Depew, Kevin. *Five Things You Need to Know: More People, More Risk.* Retrieved February 9, 2008 from
http://www.minyanville.com/articles/index.php?a=15849

119. Stevens, Allison. "Stimulus Plan Falls Short in Female-Friendly Audit." *Women's Enews*, Retrieved February 3, 2008 from
http://www.womensenews.org/article.cfm?aid=3479

120. Ibid.

121. "Fact Sheet: Women and Unemployment Insurance: Outdated Rules Deny Benefits That Workers Need and Have Earned." Washington, D.C.: Institute for Women's Policy Research, January, 2008.

122. U.S. Social Security Act, §510(b)(2).

123. Platner, John. *Planned Parenthood, Bush and Birth Control.*(2005). Retrieved February 18, 2008 from
http://www.plannedparenthood.org/issues-action/birth-control/bc-bush-6516.htm

124. ABC News. *Abstinence Only' Sex Ed Ineffective.* (April 2007). Retrieved February 18, 2008 from
http://abcnews.go.com/Health/Sex/story?id=3048738

125. Stobbe, Mike."Teen Birthrate Makes Rare Rise." Associated Press, Thursday, Dec. 6, 2007.

126. Kevles, Daniel J. "The Secret History of Birth Control." *New York Times*, July 22, 2001.

127. Gold, Rachel Benson. "Federal Authority to Impose Medicaid Family Planning Cuts: A Deal States Should Refuse." *Guttmacher Policy Review,* Spring 2006: Volume 9, Number 2.

128. NARAL Pro-Choice America. *Global Gag Rule: A Flawed Policy That Sacrifices Women's Lives.* (January 2007) Retrieved December 22, 2007 from http://www.prochoiceamerica.org/issues/abortion/

129. Goldberg, Carey. "Insurance for Viagra Spurs Coverage for Birth Control." *New York Times*, June 30, 1999.

130. Hunte,r Kathleen. *Poor may lose taxpayer-funded Viagra.* (June 2005). Retrieved December 22, 2007 from www.stateline.org

131. Stein, Rob. "Pharmacists' Rights at Front Of New Debate." *Washington Post*, March 28, 2005: A01.

132. Our Bodies, Ourselves Health Resource Center. *History of Abortion in the U.S.*" Retrieved December 22, 2007 from http://www.ourbodiesourselves.org

133. National Abortion Federation. *History of Abortion.* Retrieved December 22, 2007 from http://www.prochoice.org

134. Ibid.

135. *Naf Violence And Disruption Statistics: Incidents of Violence & Disruption Against Abortion Providers in The U.S. & Canada.* Retrieved February 18, 2008 from www.prochoice.org

136. Democracy Now. *Ashcroft Seeks Hospital Abortion Records.* (February 13, 2004). Retrieved December 22, 2007 from http://www.democracynow.org

137. "Abortion Access in the United States," *Choice Voices,* Planned Parenthood of New York City, February, 2007.

138. American Civil Liberties Union. *Timeline of Important Reproductive Freedom Cases Decided by the Supreme Court.* Retrieved December 31, 2007 from http://www.aclu.org

139. Ibid.

140. Guttmacher Institute. *Abortion Policy in the Absence of Roe, State Policies in Brief.* Retrieved December 1, 2007 from http://www.guttmacher.org

141. "Abortion Foes Focus on States," *Feminist Daily News Wire,* January 14, 2008.

142. *Voters Real Health Care Agenda.* Retrieved January 8, 2008 from http://justice.org/pressroom/CJSPollMe

143. AARP. *Affordable Health Care.* Retrieved January 3, 2008 from DividedWeFail.org

144. "National Report: Women's Access to Health Care Services." Washington, D.C.: National Women's Law Center, 2007.

145. Ibid.

146. U.S. Center for Disease Control, National Center for Health Statistics. *Child Health*. (2006). Retrieved January 4, 2008 from http://www.cdc.gov

147. Gonzalez, Veronica. "Rising drug prices taking toll at UNCW." *StarNewsOnline*, September 10, 2007. Retrieved January 3, 2008 from http://www.starnewsonline.com

148. Hitti, Miranda. "AARP: Prescription Drug Prices Up." *WebMD Medical News*, March 6, 2007.

149. "Senate kills bid to import prescription drugs." The Associated Press, May 7, 2007.

150. "The High Cost of Health Care," *New York Times*, November 25, 2007: A9.

151. "Policy Briefing: Expanding Access To Affordable Health Care." Romney for President Campaign, Aug 24, 2007. Retrieved January 5, 2008 from http://www.mittromney.com

152. "Doctors Give Massachusetts Health Reform a Failing Grade." *North Denver News*, January 10 2008.

153. *Definition of Socialized Medicine*. Retrieved January 8, 2008 from Medicinenet.com

154. "Doctors Give Massachusetts Health Reform a Failing Grade."

155. Financial Web. *Medicare Advantage Coverage.* Retrieved January 8, 2008 from `http://www.finweb.com`

156. Barry, Patricia. "Don't Fall for the Hard Sell." *The AARP Bulletin*, October, 2007.

157. "Lame Duck Budget.". *New York Times*, February 5, 2008.

158. *Lawmakers are Seeking Legislation That Addresses Medicare Part D Problems.* (August, 2006). Retrieved January 8, 2008 from `NeedyMeds.com`

159. Institute for America's Future. *Falling Through the Doughnut Hole.* (June 2006). Retrieved January 8, 2008 from `outfuture.org`

160. Center for Medicare Advocacy. *2008 Part D Coverage - Major Changes Are Coming.* Retrieved November 1, 2007 from `http://www.medicareadvocacy.org`

161. "Fiscal Year 2004 Federal MSIS Tables." U.S. Centers for Medicare and Medicaid Services, June 2007.

162. Pear, Robert."U.S. Curtailing Bids to Expand Medicaid Rolls." *New York Times*, January 4, 2008: A1.

163. The Henry J. Kaiser Family Foundation. *Women's Health Insurance Coverage Fact Sheet.* Retrieved December 7, 2007 from `http://www.kff.org`

164. Lambrew, Jeanne M., Ph.D."The State Children's Health Insurance Program: Past, Present, and Future." The Commonwealth Fund, February 9, 2007, Volume 49.

165. Mallaby, Sebastian."Bush's Unhealthy Veto."
Washington Post, Monday, October 1, 2007: A19.

166. Physicians for a National Health Program. *1.8 Million Veterans Lack Health Coverage*. Retrieved November 30, 2007 from `http://www.pnhp.org`

167. Greenstein, Robert, Peter Orszag and Richard Kogan."The Implications of the Social Security Projections Issued by The Congressional Budget Office." Washington, D.C.: Center on Budget and Policy Priorities, 2004.

168. "Mass Confusion." *AARP Magazine*, November/ December 2007.

169. Ibid.

170. United States Social Security Administration. *Social Security Is Important to Women*. (October, 2007). Retrieved December 15, 2008 from `http://www.socialsecurity.gov/pressoffice/ factsheets/women.htm`

171. "Six Key Facts on Women and Social Security Fact Sheet." Washington, D.C.: Institute for Women's Policy Research, May 2005.

172. United States Social Security Administration. *Social Security Is Important to Women*.

173. United States Social Security Administration. *Social Security Is Important to Women*.

174. "Six Key Facts on Women and Social Security Fact Sheet."

175. Krugman, Paul. "Good sense from the CBO," *New York Times Online*, November 9, 2007, 7:34 pm.

176. Economic Policy Institute. *Economic Snapshots.* (February 17, 2005). Retrieved November 9, 2007 from http://www.epinet.org

177. *Reimagining America, AARP's Blueprint for the Future*. Washington, D.C.: AARP, 2005.

178. *Strengthening Social Security for Women.* Washington, D.C.:Task Force on Women and Social Security, National Council of Women's Organizations and the Institute for Women's Policy Research, 1999.

179. Ibid.

180. *Reimagining America, AARP's Blueprint for the Future.*

181. Ibid.

182. *Strengthening Social Security for Women.*

183. U.S. Department of Health and Human Services, National Clearinghouse for Long-term Care Information, 2007. Retrieved Jan. 4, 2008 from http://www.longtermcare.gov

184. Tolchin, Martin. "Other Countries Do Much More for Disabled." *New York Times*, March 29, 1990.

185. Baker, Beth."Home, Sweet Nursing Home." *Ms.* magazine, Spring, 2007.

186. Ibid.

187. "AARP's Strategic Plan." Washington, D.C.: AARP. April, 2006.

188. Heymann, Jody, Alison Earle, Jeffrey Hayes. "How Does the United States Measure Up?" Institute for Health and Social Policy, McGill University, 2007.

189. HR 1542, Healthy Families Act, introduced by Rep. Rosa DeLauro, 110th Congress of the United States.

190. Vestal, Christine. *Sick leave tops state labor agendas.* Retrieved January 4, 2007 from `http://www.statel ine.org`

191. "U.S. stands apart from other nations on maternity leave." The Associated Press, July 26, 2005.

192. Jeffrey A. Mello. *Defining Hours of Service Under the Family and Medical Leave Act in Employment Disputes.* Retrieved February 16, 2008 from `http://64.233.167.104/search?q=cache:Bmjax 8tzhEsJ:www.cba.csus.edu/Partner/media/jou rnal/FMLA%2520paper%2520for%2520Journal.do c+Family+Medical+Leave+Jeffrey+A.+Mello+To wson&hl=en&ct=clnk&cd=1&gl=us`

193. Heyman et. al.

194. Heyman et. al.

195. Department of Professional Employees, AFL-CIO. *Professional Women: Vital Statistics Fact Sheet 2007.* Retrieved January 2, 2008 from `http://www.dpeaflcio.org`

196. Organisation for Economic Co-operation and Development. *Can Parents Afford to Work? Childcare costs, tax-benefit policies and work incentives.* (January

2006.) Retrieved November 15, 2007 from
http://www.oecd.org/dataoecd/35/43/35969537.pdf

197. Ibid.

198. Helburn, Suzanne W. and Barbara R. Bergmann. *America's Child Care Problem.* New York: Palgrave, 2002.

199. *pre[k]now, National Fact Sheet.* (2007). Retrieved January 15, 2008 from
http://www.preknow.org/advocate/factsheets/snapshot.cfm

200. *Putting the Annual Cost of the War in Perspective.* Retrieved Feb. 19, 2008 from
http://www.nytimes.com

201. *Child Care in America.* (2007). Retrieved January 15, 2008 from
http://www.naccrra.org/news/program.php?Page=6

202. Retrieved January 15, 2008 from
http://zfacts.com/p/716.html#3033

203. Payscale.com. *Median Hourly Rate by City - Job: Child Care / Day Care Worker (United States).* Retrieved January 15, 2008 from
http://www.payscale.com/research

204. Smith, Kristin and Reagan Baughman. "Low Wages Prevalent in Direct Care and Child Care Workforce." Carsey Institute, University of New Hampshire, Summer, 2007.

205. Helburn and Bergmann.

206. Helburn and Bergmann.

207. National Association for the Education of Young Children. *Child Care and Development Block Grant*." Retrieved January 15, 2008 from
http://www.naeyc.org

208. Mezey, Parrott, Greenberg, and Fremstad. "Reversing Direction on Welfare Reform: President's Budget Cuts Child Care for 300,000 Children." Center on Budget and Policy Priorities, Center for Law and Social Policy, 2004.

209. "U.S. Child Care Seriously Lags Behind that of Europe." *American Sociological Association News*, November 18, 2002.

210. Helburn and Bergmann.

211. Belasco.

212. Musil, Caryn McTigue. "Scaling the Ivory Towers." *Ms.* magazine, Fall 2007.

213. Mather, Mark and Dia Adams. *The Crossover in Female-Male College Enrollment Rates*. (February 7, 2007). Retrieved January 19, 2008 from http://www.prb.org

214. Musil.

215. Musil.

216. Feminist Majority Foundation. *Education Equality*. Retrieved January, 15, 2008 from
http://feminist.org/education/

217. National Women's Law Center. *Report Confirms Clarification Weakens Title IX.* (March, 2006). Retrieved January 15, 2008 from `http://www.nwlc.org`

218. Homer, Liz, Sue Klein, and Jan Erickson. "Dangers of Using Title IX to Increase Sex Segregation in U.S. Public Education." Unpublished paper. Washington, D.C.: National Association of Women and Girls in Education, 2007.

219. Ibid.

220. Ibid.

221. Ibid.

222. National Education Association. *Urge Congress to Support Bills to Improve NCLB.* Retrieved January, 15, 2008 from `www.nea.org`

223. Estes, Ralph. *Who Pays, Who Profits?* Washington, D.C.: IPS Books, 1993.

224. "Overview of the Federal Tax System," Congressional Research Service, April, 2007.

225. Estes.

226. Estes.

227. "CTJ"'s Bush Tax Cut Scorecard: Phase-In dates for the Bush tax cuts, including 2006 legislation (calendar years)." Washington, D.C.:Citizens for Tax Justice, October 13, 2006.

228. Andrews, Edmund L."Bush Tax Cuts Offer Most For Very Rich, Study Finds." *New York Times*, January 7,

2007: A 16.

229. Weisman, Jonathan."Senate Passes Corporate Tax Bill." *Washington Post*,Tuesday, October 12, 2004: A01.

230. "Tax Cuts, Myths and Realities," Washington, D.C.: Center on Budget and Policy Priorities, November, 2007.

231. Ibid.

232. Ibid.

233. "Europe's welfare states." *The Economist*, Apil 1, 2004 .

234. Estes.

235. *Federal Estate Tax Background, Estate Tax Repeal Looks Unlikely as of August 2007.* (August 2007). Retrieved December 22, 2007 from http://www.results.org/website/article.asp?id=2022

236. Burk, Martha. "A Feminist Tea Party?" *Ms.* magazine, Spring, 2007.

237. Burk, Martha. "Money Talks, But Voters Don't Always Listen." *Ms.* magazine, Winter 2007.

238. National Committee on Pay Equity. *Census statistics show Wage Gap unchanged.* Retrieved January 20, 2008 from http://www.pay-equity.org/

239. AFL-CIO. *Working Women Fast Facts.* Retrieved January 20, 2008 from http://www.aflcio.org/issues/jobseconomy/women/upload/women.pdf

240. *Behind the Pay Gap.* Washington, D.C.: American Association of University Women Foundation, April, 2007.

241. Rose, Stephen J. and Heidi I. Hartmann."Still a Man's Labor Market: The long-term earnings gap." Washington, D.C.: Institute for Women's Policy Research, May, 2004.

242. U.S. Department of Labor, Bureau of Labor Statistics."Highlights of Women's Earnings in 2002." Report 972: September 2003.

243. "Minimum Wage: Facts at a Glance." Washington, D.C.: Economic Policy Institute, April, 2007.

244. Ibid.

245. "Behind the Pay Gap."

246. "Women's Policy Agenda," Website and speeches, Bill Richardson for President, 2007.
`richardsonforpresident.com`

247. *Adarand Construction v. Pena.* The Court ruled that the most rigorous type of constitutional review, "strict scrutiny," must be applied to federal affirmative action programs. At the same time it ruled that affirmative action programs are both legal and needed.

248. Moore, Mary and Jennifer Hahn."Contracting Connerly." *Ms.* magazine, Winter 2008.

249. Ocampo, Carmina. "Prop 209: Ten Long Years." *The Nation*, December 11, 2006.

250. Wilfore, Kristina. "Take the Initiative: A feminist guide to ballot measures that will impact women's lives." *Ms.* magazine, Fall 2006.

251. Ibid.

252. News of the Nation. *Affirmative Action Setbacks* (1997). Retrieved December 29, 2007 from `Infoplease.com`

253. Moore and Hahn.

254. Walker, Blair S. *Washington's Anti-Affirmative Action Vote Thrust Into Spotlight.* (July 13, 1999). Retrieved December 29, 2007 from `Stateline.org`

255. Kaufmann, Susan W. "The Potential Impact of the Michigan Civil Rights Initiative on Employment, Education and Contracting." The University of Michigan: Center for the Education of Women, June 2006.

256. Lopez, Kathryn Jean. "Come On People." *National Review Online*, November 26, 2007.

257. Goldberg Day, Judy and Catherine Hill. *Behind the Pay Gap.* Washington, D.C.: American Association of University Women Educational Foundation, 2007.

258. "2007 Catalyst Census of Women Board Directors of the Fortune 500," New York: Catalyst, 2007.

259. Simon, Stephanie."Affirmative re-action."*Los Angeles Times*, January 19, 2008.

260. Zwahlen, Cyndia. "SBA Effort for Women Owners Stirs Outrage." *Los Angeles Times*, January 3, 2008.

261. "Women Business Owners and Their Enterprises." Washington, D.C.: National Women's Business Council, July, 2007.

262. U.S. Women's Chamber of Commerce. Retrieved February 22, 2008 from `http://www.uswcc.org/`

263. American Bar Association, citing U.S. Department of Justice, Patricia Tjaden & Nancy Thoennes. *Extent, Nature, and Consequences of Intimate Partner Violence* (2000). Retrieved December 15, 2007 from `http://www.ojp.usdoj.gov/nij/pubs-sum/1818` `67.htm`

264. Ibid.

265. American Bar Association, citing The Violence Policy Center. *When Men Murder Women: An Analysis of 2002 Homicide Data: Females Murdered by Males in Single Victim/Single Offender Incidents.* (2004). Retrieved December 14, 2007 from `http://www.vpc.org/studies/wmmw2004.pdf`

266. American Bar Association, citing Matthew R. Durose et al., U.S. Department of Justice Bureau of Justice Statistics. *Family Violence Statistics: Including Statistics on Strangers and Acquaintances.* (2005). Retrieved December 14, 2007 from `http://www.ojp.usdoj.gov/bjs/pub/pdf/fvs.p` `df`

267. "Maze of Injustice: The Failure to Protect Indigenous Women from Sexual Violence in the USA." Washington, D.C.: Amnesty International, 2007.

268. National Coalition to End Domestic Violence. *FY 2008 Appropriations, Violence Against Women Act (VAWA).* Retrieved December 22, 2007from

http://www.ncadv.org

269. National Organization for Women. *Put Volunteer Attorneys to Work for Domestic Violence Survivors.* Retrieved January 21, 2008 from http://www.capwiz.com/now/issues/alert/?al ertid=10543461

270. Zogby Poll. *"Don't Ask, Don't Tell" Not Working.* (December 18, 2006). Downloaded February 22, 2008 from http://zogby.com/news

271. Ibid.

272. Gay & Lesbian Alliance Against Defamation. *Focus: Public Opinion & Polls.* Retrieved January 5, 2008 from http://www.glaad.org/

273. "Election 2006: Support for same-sex marriage grows significantly." Washington, D.C.: National Gay and Lesbian Task Force, November 08, 2006.

274. Unpublished data provided to the author by The Pew Research Center for People and the Press, February, 2008.

275. "Less Opposition to Gay Marriage, Adoption and Military Service." Washington, D.C.: The Pew Research Center for People and the Press, March 22, 2006.

276. Gallup poll, May, 2005, cited by *Focus: Public Opinion & Polls.*

277. Jackson, Derrick Z."Optimism in the hate crimes debate." *The Boston Globe*, May 26, 2007: A11.

278. "Confronting Rape in the Military," *New York Times*, March 12, 2004.

279. Ibid.

280. Risen, James. "U.S. women reporting rapes in Iraq remain in limbo," *International Herald Tribune*, February 13, 2008.

281. Center for Reproductive Rights. *Penalized For Serving Their Country: The Ban On Abortion For Women In the Military*. (June 2003). Retrieved January 2, 2008 from http://www.reproductiverights.org

282. Tyson, Ann Scott."For Female GIs, Combat Is a Fact." *Washington Post*, Friday, May 13, 2005: A01.

283. "Women's Movement Worthwhile." CBS News Poll October 2005.

284. "Female Veterans Return Home, Find Services Lacking," National Public Radio: *Talk of the Nation*. July 24, 2007.

285. "RAND Study Finds Divorce Among Soldiers Has Not Spiked Higher Despite Stress Created By Battlefield Deployments." The RAND Corporation, April 12, 2007.

286. NARAL Pro-Choice America. *Global Gag Rule: A Flawed Policy That Sacrifices Women's Lives*. (January 22,2007). Retrieved December 15, 2007 from http://www.prochoiceamerica.org

287. *Human Rights for All, CEDAW*. Leila Rassekh Milani (ed.). Washington, D.C.: Working Group on Ratification of the U.N. Convention on the Elimination of All Forms of Discrimination Against Women, 2001.

288. United States Campaign to Ban Landmines. *The Mine Ban Treaty and the US Government: 10 Years and*

Waiting. Retrieved December 1, 2007 from
http://www.banminesusa.org/

289. UNICEF. *Convention on the Rights of the Child
(CRC).* Retrieved December 1, 2007 from
http://www.unicef.org

290. U.S. Department of State. *Bush Calls Women's
Rights and Liberty "Inseparable."* (March 12, 2004).
Retrieved January 3, 2008 from
http://usinfo.state.gov/sa/Archive/2004/Ma
r/15-507261.html

291. 'Wave Of Violence' Against Women In Iraq," NBC
Nightly News, November 23, 2007.

292. "Taliban Attacks on Afghan Girls' Schools
Increase," *Feminist Daily News Wire,* July 12, 2006.

293. Whitaker, Brian. "Taliban murders voters to derail
election," London: *The Guardian,* June 28, 2004.

294. Amnesty International. *Tell Secretary of State Rice:
No More Delays in Darfur.* Retrieved January 30, 2008
from http://takeaction.amnestyusa.org

295. Burk, Martha. *Cult of Power: Sex discrimination in
corporate America and what can be done about it.* New
York: Scribner, 2005, p. 83.

Index

Index

1519219

Made in the USA